Where Is the Way?

Humanistic Buddhism for Everyday Life

WHERE IS THE WAY?

Humanistic Buddhism for Everyday Life

Venerable Master Hsing Yun

Edited by Joyce Meadows

Fo Guang Shan International Translation Center

© 2015 Fo Guang Shan International Translation Center

By Venerable Master Hsing Yun
Edited by Joyce Meadows
Cover Photo: Zhong Min Peng
Cover Design: Rachel Xu
Book Design: Xiaoyang Zhang

Fo Guang Shan International Translation Center
3456 Glenmark Drive
Hacienda Heights, CA 91745, U.S.A.
Tel: (626) 330-8361
Fax: (626) 330-8363
E-mail: info@fgsitc.org
Website: www.fgsitc.org

Printed in Taiwan.
18 17 16 15 14   1 2 3 4 5

Library of Congress Cataloging-in-Publication Data

Xingyun, 1927-
  [Works. Selections. English]
  Where is the way : humanistic Buddhism for everyday life / written by
Venerable Master Hsing Yun ; edited by Joyce Meadows. -- First edition.
     pages cm
  ISBN 978-1-943211-02-9 (pbk.)
  1. Humanistic Buddhism. 2. Fo Guang Shan Buddhist Order--Doctrines. I.
Meadows, Joyce, 1952- editor. II. Title.
  BQ9800.F6392X552 2015
  294.3'444--dc23
                          2015014176

Contents

Acknowledgements

Foreword: Lewis Lancaster   i

Introduction   v

PART I   WAKING UP

One   On The Four Noble Truths: The Way of What the
Buddha Taught   3

Two   On Cause and Effect: The Way of Dependent
Origination   21

Three   On Knowledge: The Way of Study   31

Four   On Religion: The Way of Faith   37

PART II   LIVING IN THE WORLD

Five   On Emotions: The Way of Love and Affection   45

Six   On Loving-kindness and Compassion: The Way of
Becoming a Bodhisattva   51

Seven   On Ethics and Morality: The Way of Cultivating
Affinity   59

Eight   On Society: The Way of Oneself and Others   65

PART III   STAYING ON THE WAY

Nine   On Education and Entertainment: The Way of
            Mindful Living   77

Ten   On Long Life, Wealth, and Happiness: The Way of
            Ownership   89

Eleven   On Government and International Affairs:
            The Way of Tolerance   99

Twelve   On Nature: The Way of Environmental Protection   109

            PART IV   MOVING FORWARD ON
                      THE DHARMA JOURNEY

Thirteen   On the Triple Gem Ceremony: The Way of
            Becoming a Buddhist   121

Fourteen   On the Five Precepts: The Way of Beginning
            the Path   135

Fifteen   On Buddhism and Democratic Principles:
            The Way of Freedom   147

Sixteen   On the Future: The Way of Development   155

Conclusion   Living Our Vows: The Way of Happiness   167

GLOSSARY OF NAMES AND TERMS

GLOSSARY OF SUTRAS AND TEXTS

ACKNOWLEDGEMENTS

Like all of Fo Guang Shan International Translation Center's endeavors, this project benefited from the contribution of many people. We would like to thank Venerable Tzu Jung, the president of the Fo Guang Shan International Translation Center (FGSITC), Venerable Yi Chao, Executive Director of FGSITC, Venerable Miao Hsi, and Venerable Hui Dong, Abbot of Hsi Lai Temple, for their support and leadership.

John Balcom provided the translation; Joyce Meadows edited the texts; Dr. Lewis Lancaster wrote the foreward; and Natalie Lauren Morales, Amanda Ling, and Xiaoyang Zhang proofread the manuscript and prepared it for publication.

Our appreciation goes to everyone who supported this project from conception to completion.

FOREWORD

Reading this volume is like sitting with Master Hsing Yun. It is as if we listen in to what he says as he meets an unending file of visitors, each wanting to have a moment of his time and wisdom. His flow of teaching comes without resistance. Through the years, as I have watched him teach, I realize that he does not sigh. He does not show boredom or weariness with the hours of meeting and talking to his audiences whether of hundreds or just one individual. Listening to him always seems to be an occasion to hear a revelation just about what he thinks and feels. On the surface, it seems so simple and lucid that it is easy to miss the complexity of his thoughts. However, when the voice is put into words, as in this book, we can note a wide range of topics, references, quotes, statements by other teachers, textual sources, and literary allusions. He has the ability to deliver these words without notes or other memory aids. His phenomenal memory when giving a public presentation makes it appear that what he is doing is easy. Recently at a conference at Fo Guang Shan, he addressed every presenter and gave his thanks for their past accomplishments, publications, and research areas. In an auditorium filled with attendees, we watched with wonder as the number grew to more than 25 scholars from eight nations and yet he never stumbled or made a wrong identification. It was spontaneous and without any assistance, no cards, no computer screen. Those who witnessed this amazing flow of information could hardly fathom the depth of his memory or the sharpness of his recall. When someone mentioned their amazement, he told us that when he was young he had a very limited memory and was often punished for being behind others. Then, one morning, he awoke and his memory had changed and he could remember everything he had read or heard. He still has this ability and it can be seen in the text of this volume where he has spoken the recorded words without aids of any kind. The flow seems so unpracticed and yet the very ease and simplicity is a sign of a master teacher who has full control of his message and delivery. When he tells us that he will cover eight aspects of a theme, we can keep track and see that in fact he always discusses all eight in the correct order.

In one sense what is written here is not for the faint-of-heart. He tells us that suffering must be recognized, that, at times, it is impossible to avoid the forces of nature, that we must focus on our own faults, and that we often live with those who dislike us. There is truthfulness in the discussion about our lives and the problems we face, the fears we feel about the menace of the future and the potential of disaster from forces and influences beyond our control.

In another sense, what is written here is precisely for the faint-of-heart. While we cannot avoid the realities of illness, old age, and death, the Buddhist message shows us how we can overcome these realities with the hope of cessation of suffering and the path that leads us away from it. This approach does not ask us to live in denial but to have full consciousness of our situation. In a step-by-step method of learning or training, we can transform emotions that are destructive, to ones that nurture. We can come to rely on those who are "Bodhi-sattvas" among us in our everyday life. The Master turns us from the idea that Bodhisattvas only exist is another plane of existence, distant and god-like. Instead, he says, we can find them all around us ready to provide wisdom that gives us a new fearlessness in the face of the greatest of problems.

When our fear abates, we can use a different lens to view our world. That lens is "oneness". We are interlocked with everyone around us. This is the antidote to such evils as the Holocaust or efforts to have ethnic cleansing through death and destruction. Such a lens keeps us from racist rhetoric and actions and rejection of those who seem to be "different". Once these insights come to us, and with them compassion for others who suffer as we do ourselves, the next step is to set a course of cultivation. This training starts with "vows" that are made real through learning and study and contemplation. Our actions become "fully conscious", they are intentional and not just accidental. These vows become our guides and reminders of what we want to accomplish. Because of them, there is no reluctance to live in an environment of mutual assistance.

I know that the works of Master Hsing Yun are numerous and I began to wonder about the best way for people to make use of this newest volume. As I pondered this question, I had an opportunity to meet my son, Dr. Linus Lancaster, for coffee and one of our periodic sharings of work and research. He gave me a new insight, and with his permission, I share it. When we read or hear the words of others, it is an act of "listening". If we can focus completely on "listening" rather than allowing our thoughts to wander or create our own words that will be used when we speak, this perfecting of "listening" becomes a spiritual practice. Our minds are free of our own thoughts and we move away from ego centric actions. As we "listen" with this openness the act becomes an "offering"... to the words we hear and to the person who is speaking them.

Reading and "listening" to the message in this volume for a period of time can be a meditative experience. If I "vow" to listen without the interruption of my own words, I like to think that I will be giving an "offering" to the message as well as to Master Hsing Yun as he shares his insights and wisdom. He maintains that the result will lead to joy.

— Lewis Lancaster Ph.D
Professor (Emeritus),
University of California, Berkeley
Former President of University of the West

INTRODUCTION

Once Upon a Time in the Saha World

All people love a good story. We want to be entertained, enthralled, and swept away on the wings of our imaginations. We believe that we deserve a break, someone to soothe our wounded egos, something to make us feel better. We just want to feel better! So we continue to ply our well-worn, comfortable habits, searching for that perfect solution that we believe must be out there in the world. Surely if we can find it, our next story will have a happier ending.

Yet if we are truly honest with ourselves, we will admit that our lives more often resemble a circus, complete with roller coasters and endless, spinning merry-go-rounds. This is why we are drawn to books about the Dharma. This is, perhaps, why you picked up this book. We all want to find an exit to the circus. And as human beings we possess this potential, a potential that can be realized as we uncover our own Buddha nature. Like Prince Siddhartha over 2,500 years ago, we can choose to walk through the streets of our reality and do our best to alleviate suffering wherever we encounter it, for ourselves and for others.

In *Where Is the Way: Humanistic Buddhism for Everyday Life*, Master Hsing Yun gives us a blueprint for an involved life, a life in which we not only study the Buddha's teachings but also wear those teachings in each moment and with every breath. He demonstrates how we can create new stories for our lives, finding happiness throughout rather than in fleeting, punctuated moments. In short, the book lays out an active, progressive practice that is one with life and fueled by compassion.

To this effort, the book's design utilizes a methodology that is at once educational and spiritual and appeals to us as individuals as well as citizens of the world. The sixteen chapters are divided into four sections, each section building upon its predecessor as the book progresses from a personal to a global perspective. And within each chapter, Master Hsing Yun elaborates upon and illustrates the theme of Humanistic Buddhism with an inspiration born of his years of investigating, practicing, and spreading the Buddha's teachings. His explanations and insights blend the traditions of Buddhism and Chinese culture with the cross-cultural experiences of Fo Guang Shan temples and organizations across the globe.

Part I, "Waking Up," gives us an overview of Buddhism's central concepts as a foundation upon which to develop insight into their practical application as the book proceeds. That being said, it is important to state that this book is not only for the novice student, but for anyone who wishes to delve more deeply into the ideas of Humanistic Buddhism. Reading, then revisiting the Buddha's teachings time and again is like studying a fine painting. Each experience brings a fresh perspective that moves us a bit further along the path to insight.

Keep this thought in mind as you read the following encapsulations of the chapters included in Part I. Simple though they might appear, do not be deceived. These catchphrases not only foreshadow each chapter's content, but also act as springboards to a richer understanding of the Dharma. In approaching Chapter One "On the Four Noble Truths" think, reality uncovered. This chapter presents the Buddha's first teaching which serves as the cornerstone for all of his subsequent teachings. In approaching Chapter Two "On Cause and Effect" think, choices and connections. In approaching Chapter Three "On Knowledge" think, heart and mind. And finally, in approaching Chapter Four "On Religion" think, community and practice. Each chapter adds another piece to the puzzle that comprises the nature of suffering while giving us the insights to transform that suffering into wisdom and compassion.

Part II, "Living in the World," carries us forward on the wings of the Dharma. The insights from Part I become stepping stones in our exploration of bringing the Buddha's teachings into our everyday world. Master Hsing Yun facilitates our investigation by presenting "slice of life" situations in which the light of Humanistic Buddhism pervades common activities and interactions. The chapters included in Part II, therefore, teach us about conduct, the nature of relationships, and the taking and accepting of responsibility. In each chapter Master Hsing Yun imparts knowledge and wisdom by way of the Buddha's teachings, historical example, and personal experience, leading us to reflect upon the possibilities for our own lives as individuals, family members, and citizens.

Chapter Five, "On Emotions," asks us to consider the meaning of love without clinging and the offering of compassion without restriction. Chapter Six, "On Loving-kindness and Compassion," asks us to investigate the meaning and necessity of wisdom. Chapter Seven, "On Ethics and Morality" beckons us to uncover the ways in which we can use the previous chapters' insights as guidelines for healthy and respectful relationships. Lastly, Chapter Eight, "On Society," asks what is needed from us to promote harmony in the societies that we call home.

If Part II speaks to us of responsibility to ourselves, our families, and our societies, Part III "Staying on the Way," challenges us to discern the qualities of a rewarding life within the context of the Buddha's teachings. How do we construct a mindful and compassionate existence, a happy existence while continually navigating the discordant seas of our relationships and material life? Master Hsing Yun first addresses these issues on an individual level, giving us food for thought about our personal conduct. Through cultural examples and guidance from the Buddha's teachings, he, then, extends the focus of this question to include interactions with our local civic communities, our nations, and finally, with global society.

Chapter Nine, "On Education and Entertainment," encourages us to look beyond our tired routines to find the extraordinary in the mundane, the diamonds in the dust of our lives. Chapter Ten, "On Long Life, Wealth, and Happiness," encourages us to write new definitions of achievement and attainment, informed by wisdom rather than greed and truth rather than ignorance. Chapter Eleven, "On Government and International Affairs," encourages us to embrace the emptiness of our differences in order to build more equitable local and global societies, drawing open mindedness out of fear, compassionate action out of violence. And not to be placed on the back burner, Chapter Twelve, "On Nature," encourages us to hold the necessity of environmental stewardship in our humanistic practice, viewing interdependence as a survival strategy, and discord as creative potential.

The final section of the book, Part IV, "Moving Forward on the Dharma Journey," gives us practical insights to inform our spiritual practice. The chapters address the steps to formalize our practice, to understand the nature of spiritual diligence, and to walk with our practice into a hopeful future. What does it mean to become a Buddhist? How do we wear the Buddha's teachings, and what are our guiding stars?

Chapter Thirteen, "On the Triple Gem Ceremony," details this formal Buddhist action of making vows, inviting us to take our first step onto the Way. Chapter Fourteen, "On the Five Precepts," presents us with our guiding stars, gifting us with the means to remain on the Way. Chapter Fifteen, "On Buddhism and Democratic Principles," outlines the freedom found within Buddhist practice, calling us to uncover the profound equanimity embedded in the Way. And lastly, Chapter Sixteen, "On the Future," explains the Buddhist conceptualizations of knowing, beckoning us to explore our future through the path.

At first glance, it might appear that this book poses more questions than it answers. You think, "Now wait just a minute, answers are why I picked up a book about Humanistic Buddhism in the first place." Yet if we quiet our minds and let go of our presumptions, we will begin to see that through the Buddha's teachings, Master Hsing Yun has, indeed, given us the only answer that we need, an answer that has been with us all along. The answer to all of our questions is quite simply, us. This book, *Where Is the Way: Humanistic Buddhism for Everyday Life* acts as a mirror reflecting our own Buddha nature, a tool to uncover life's answers from within ourselves.

So welcome, the gate to the Way is wide open.

— Editor,
Joyce Meadows

PART I

Waking Up

The real treasure of energy is not in
the mountains or in the oceans,

but in one's own mind;

the real treasure of the Dharma is not in
the sutras or in the mouth,

but in one's own mind.

— *Humble Table, Wise Fair*
Inspirtation

Chapter One

On the Four Noble Truths:
The Way of What the Buddha Taught

The value of learning the Dharma is not something that can be easily measured. The first step we must take when we enter the gate of the Dharma is to look at ourselves. We must decide that we want to change, that we want to learn, and that we will sincerely attempt to apply the Buddha's teachings in our daily lives. The moment we embrace the Dharma, our lives will begin to change. The Dharma is like a light that dispels the darkness.

Following his awakening, the Buddha first gave the teaching of the Four Noble Truths to the group of five monks at the Deer Park on the outskirts of Benares. He was thirty-five years old. The Buddha dedicated his earthly life to teaching the Dharma, leaving his disciples a profound legacy. The Four Noble Truths became the fundamental teachings of Buddhism. They were realized, experienced, and taught by the Buddha himself, and encapsulate the true nature of life and the universe.

The Four Noble Truths also form the foundation of Buddhism from which all Buddhist sutras derive. In this context, the word "truth" implies the investigation and examination of reality, while the word "suffering" is a standard English translation of the Sanskrit word *dukkha*, meaning unsatisfactory. The Four Noble Truths are truth of suffering, the truth of the causes of suffering, the truth of the cessation of suffering, and the truth of the path leading to the cessation of suffering.

The Significance of the Four Noble Truths

The word noble refers to righteousness. According to the sutras, "The noble are also righteous and they apply righteousness in all matters. This is what is called noble." The meaning of the word "truth" in the Four Noble Truths is further explained in the *Stages of Yogacara Practice Treatise*: "From the truth of suffering to the truth of the path leading to the cessation of suffering, it is all true, not upside down. Thus it is called truth." In other words, the Four Noble Truths are incontrovertible. Additionally, the *Commentary on the Middle Way Treatise* states, "The Four Noble Truths are the root of ignorance and enlightenment. In the state of ignorance, you will be trapped within the chaos of the six realms of existence. In the state of awakening, you will become a sage of the three vehicles."

Therefore, the Four Noble Truths stand at the core of all life. They explain all phenomena in the universe and teach us the means to achieve liberation from all delusions. Understanding them depends on wisdom, the wisdom to look deeply and see past our ignorance. The first truth says that life is full of suffering. The second truth says that suffering is caused by our attachments. The third truth says that awakening or complete liberation from all suffering is possible. The fourth truth teaches us how to awaken.

An additional insight involves the cause and effect relationships between the Four Noble Truths. The first truth is the effect of the second, while the third truth is the effect of the fourth. At first glance, you might wonder why the Buddha placed the truths in this particular order. It seems more logical to place the second and fourth truths, which are both causes, before the first and thirds truths, which are both effects. The Buddha chose to use a different order because he wanted to teach the Four Noble Truths in the most effective way possible. Since it is easier for most people to grasp the effect and then come to understand its causes, the Buddha placed the truth of suffering first. Then, he explained the causes of suffering. Once people understand the first two truths, they naturally want to liberate themselves from their suffering. To help us understand how to achieve liberation, the Buddha taught the third noble truth, which is the cessation of suffering. Then he taught the fourth noble truth, which is the path that leads to the cessation of suffering.

Central to all of the Buddha's teachings is the immense compassion he showed in crafting explanations that could be understood by everyone. The teaching of the Four Noble Truths is very profound, and as we learn more about the truths, we will realize how the Buddha's wisdom and compassion enabled him to teach them so clearly. Let us take a closer look.

The First Noble Truth

Suffering is the state in which the body and mind are driven by afflictions. The truth of suffering illustrates how life is full of the resulting suffering. The Buddha saw with perfect clarity that none of us can escape from this reality, and that it is not possible for a human being to achieve complete satisfaction in this world. Personally, I have always believed that we should have a happy, optimistic, and positive outlook on life. We should not constantly talk about suffering, walk around with knitted eyebrows, and be consumed with depression and misery.

The purpose of talking about suffering in Buddhism is to help us realize that all kinds of suffering exist in this world. Once we uncover the actual nature of suffering, we can take a further step and find a way to end to it. Thus, understanding the existence of suffering is only part of the process. Learning how to put an end to suffering so that we can attain liberation is the ultimate purpose of discoursing about suffering in Buddhism.

You may ask, "Why does Buddhism say that life is full of suffering? I am not hungry for fame and wealth, nor am I hampered by love and emotions. My life is filled with happiness." According to Buddhist scriptures, there are many varieties of suffering, such as the three forms of suffering, the eight types of suffering, the one hundred and eight kinds of suffering, and countless other forms. All of these sufferings can be classified into either physical or mental suffering.

Some people have little craving for material comforts: they are able to withstand the discomforts of extreme weather and accept the pain of impoverishment. Still others are able to rise above the bondage of emotions, handle the agony of being separated from loved ones, and tolerate the nuisance of dealing with people they do not like. No one, however, is free from the pain that occurs at the end of life.

Actually, it makes no difference whether we discuss it or not because everyone will experience some kind of suffering during his or her lifetime. But if we can clearly discern the origins of suffering, we can, then, find ways to free ourselves and enjoy the real happiness of life.

The "I" of Suffering

We have discussed some of the ways Buddhists understand human life as being mired in suffering. Now, we will look more deeply into the sources of suffering as we delineate some of its most basic expressions in our life. In other words, we suffer when:

1. *The self is not in harmony with the material world.* We constantly struggle to find comfort in this world. When our houses are too small and there are too many people, we feel uncomfortable. When our desk is too high or too low, the lamp is too bright or too dim, we may find it difficult to study. The material world does not revolve around us in just the way we would like, so we suffer.

2. *The self is not in harmony with other people.* All too often, rather than being with the people we wish, we are forced to spend time with people who are difficult for us to get along with. Sometimes, we are even forced to spend time with people who openly dislike us.

3. *The self is not in harmony with the body.* The body is born, grows old, weakens, and dies. The self has little or no control over this process.

4. *The self and the mind are not in harmony.* Our mind is often beyond our control. It races from one idea to the next like a wild horse. Delusional thought is the source of all of our suffering. Although we may know this, we still find it very hard to control the mind.

5. *The self and its desires are not in harmony.* There are good and bad desires. Good desires can improve the self, and even benefit others. However, if we poorly manage these desires, they may become burdens. Bad desires, such as coveting material things and being attached to physical desire, create more suffering. We may understand that desire produces negative karma and suffering, but that does not mean the mind will be able to con-

trol itself easily. Self-control is difficult precisely because what we know to be best for us is not always what we most want. Yet if we do not attempt to control our desires, then the self will suffer even more.

6. *The self and its views are not in good harmony.* This basically means that we have wrong views or false perceptions. When what we believe is not in accordance with the truth, we cause ourselves endless trouble, repeating the same mistakes time and again.

7. *The self is not in harmony with nature.* Rain, floods, droughts, storms, waves, and all forces of nature are beyond our control, often causing us to suffer.

Now take heart! Despite the overwhelming nature of its existence, the Buddha taught the truth of suffering not to make us despair but to help us clearly recognize the realities of life. When we understand the extent of our suffering and the impossibility of avoiding it, we should feel inspired to overcome it. This refers to the hopefulness of the third and fourth noble truths, the possibility of the cessation of suffering and the path leading us away from our suffering.

The Second Noble Truth

In Buddhism, karma refers to all that we say, think, and do. Throughout our lives, we create a lot of unwholesome karma because of our ignorant urges and cravings. Unwholesome karma is like a seed that bears the fruit of suffering. Thus, our suffering is caused by our own karma, and we are subject to the effects of whatever actions we have done. Karma does not disappear; it only accumulates. However, karma is not all bad. There is also good karma.

Whether we taste the fruit of suffering or of joy depends on the karmic seeds that we sow.

According to the *Demonstration of Mind-Only Treatise*, "Birth and death follow each other, as a result of affliction, action, and suffering." Sentient beings are driven by the afflictions of greed, anger, and ignorance (the three poisons) and therefore accumulate various kinds of negative effects. We chain ourselves to the painful and delusive world through our strong attachments to these poisons, resulting in the never-ending cycle of birth and death.

Afflictions are referred to by many names. Afflictions are obstructions or shroudings, as they obstruct our intrinsic nature. Afflictions are knots or entanglements. Afflictions are ropes that coil around our minds. Afflictions are bindings or restraints constraining our bodies and minds. Because afflictions are not in our inherent nature, they arise and exist only through our confusion about the truths, and are thus called "momentary dust." In order to be free from afflictions, we must eliminate the causes that trigger them and avoid generating further negative karma. Should we achieve this, a blissful life is not far away. A thorough understanding of the causes of suffering is necessary before we can arrive at the extinction of suffering.

The Third Noble Truth

The cessation of suffering refers to the elimination of the afflictions of greed, anger, and ignorance, uncovering our intrinsic Buddha nature. This is nirvana. The *Explanation of the Mahayana* and the *Great Commentary on the Flower Adornment Sutra* state that, "nirvana is a Sanskrit term for cessation." Nirvana is the liberation actualized after having understood the truth of suffering and removed its cause. It is the liberation that moves beyond the confusion of afflictions and suffering, the dualities of self and others, right and wrong, and the limitations of ignorance. In other words, nirvana is a state of oneness, of freedom and ease, light and happiness, and release from the cycle of birth and death. The bliss of nirvana can be attained by anyone at any moment and is the ultimate ideal.

The Fourth Noble Truth

The Fourth Noble Truth is the truth of the path leading to the cessation of suffering. This path shows us how to overcome the causes of suffering and leads to nirvana. The most basic way to move forward in this effort is to follow the Noble Eightfold Path. Its eight steps include:

1. *Right View*: This includes developing a clear understanding of the law of cause and effect, wholesome and unwholesome karma, impermanence, suffering, and emptiness. It encompasses observations that lead us away from delusion.
2. *Right Thought*: This means to not have thoughts of greed, anger, and ignorance. It involves contemplating and distinguishing the true features of phenomena with wisdom.
3. *Right Speech*: This includes speaking words of truth, compassion, praise, and altruism.
4. *Right Action*: This includes the correct conduct of refraining from killing, stealing, engaging in sexual misconduct, and using intoxicants.
5. *Right Livelihood*: This refers to occupations and ways of making a living that do not cause harm to ourselves or to others, a harmonious, altruistic, and wholesome lifestyle.

6. *Right Effort*: This refers to the exertion of diligence in order to remain focused on advancement and not lose ground. It also means striving to do good and refraining from doing bad. In the *Great Perfection of Wisdom Treatise*, this goal includes four components: developing wholesome qualities that have not yet arisen, strengthening wholesome qualities that have already arisen, preventing unwholesome qualities that have yet to arise, and renouncing unwholesome qualities that have already arisen.

7. *Right Mindfulness*: This means to have a mind that is pure, aware, and does not give rise to unwholesome thoughts. It is contemplating the right path. There are four bases of right mindfulness: contemplate the impurities of the body, contemplate the suffering of feelings, contemplate the impermanence of the mind, and contemplate the non-selfhood of phenomena.

8. *Right Meditative Concentration*: This includes cultivating meditative concentration to focus the mind and settle the distracted body so we can better cultivate ourselves. This cultivation will reveal our Buddha nature to us.

The Importance of the Four Noble Truths

The Four Noble Truths were the first teachings of the Buddha, and they were among his last teachings. When he neared his final nirvana, the Buddha told his disciples that if any of them had doubts about the validity of the Four Noble Truths, they should speak up to have their questions answered before it was too late. The close attention that the Buddha paid to the Four Noble Truths throughout his forty-nine years of teaching shows the importance he placed on them.

When the Buddha taught the Four Noble Truths, he explained them three times from three different angles in order to aid sentient beings in their understanding of his message. These three explanations are called the "three turnings of the Dharma wheel of the Four Noble Truths with twelve aspects."

The first turning of the Dharma wheel was instructive. In this teaching, the Buddha explained the content and meaning of the Four Noble Truths so his disciples might understand their importance. He said, "Such is suffering, which is oppressive. Such is the cause of suffering, which beckons. Such is the cessation of suffering, which is attainable. Such is the path, which can be practiced."

The second turning of the Dharma wheel was to provide encouragement. In this assembly, the Buddha encouraged his disciples to put the Four Noble Truths into practice in order to eradicate their afflictions and attain liberation. The Buddha said, "Such is suffering, you should understand it. Such is the cause of suffering, you should end it. Such is the cessation of suffering, you should realize it. Such is the path, you should practice it."

In the third turning of the Dharma wheel, the Buddha shared his realization. Here, the Buddha showed his disciples that he had already realized the Four Noble Truths, and encouraged them to diligently practice so that they, too, could realize the Four Noble Truths. He said, "Such is suffering, I have understood it. Such is the cause of suffering, I have ended it. Such is the cessation of suffering, I have realized it. Such is the path, I have practiced it."

Therefore, The Four Noble Truths also explicate the relationship between life and the cosmos. The cosmos where human beings reside, known as the mundane world, is characterized by suffering and the causes of suffering. To transcend to the supramundane realm, where suffering and the cause of suffering are nonexistent, it is necessary to learn the path leading to the cessation of suffering.

The Buddha is sometimes called the "Great Doctor" because his teachings can cure us of the disease of our attachments. The best way to end suffering is to understand the Four Noble Truths. If they are properly understood, the rest of the Buddha's teachings become much easier to grasp. If the Buddha's teachings are understood and practiced, they can lead to liberation from all suffering and pain. Therefore, the Buddha is the doctor with the perfect medicine. All we need to do is take it.

Due to the significance that the Buddha placed on the Four Noble Truths, they constitute the core of all Buddhist teaching. Today, every school of Buddhism uses the Four Noble Truths as their philosophical foundation.

Development of Mahayana's Four Universal Vows

While the Four Noble Truths explain the phenomena of the universe, the Buddha expounded on them mainly as a guide for life. It is inadequate, however, to merely learn the Four Noble Truths. We must resolve, cultivate and practice accordingly. We must end the causes of suffering, practice the path, and reach the cessation of suffering in order to achieve liberation. Consequently, the Four Universal Vows and the six perfections, which are derived from the Four Noble Truths, comprise the skillful means for us to arrive at this state.

Through professing these vows, bodhisattvas aspire to benefit sentient beings and act in accord with the truth to reach this same end. Progression from the Four Noble Truths to the Four Universal Vows occurs naturally, methodically, and purposefully. And with these vows complimenting the Four Noble Truths, our own practice becomes more complete and effective, enabling us to travel the bodhisattva path of Mahayana Buddhism.

Vows

14   Where Is the Way?

If we understand suffering and its causes, yet do not vow to eliminate them, how could we claim to be cultivating ourselves to become bodhisattvas? Even if we know the infinite teachings, if we do not practice them, we will not be able to solve our problems in life, much less enter the right path. How then could we possibly fulfill the vows of bodhisattvas to attain Buddhahood?

Therefore, after understanding the Four Noble Truths, we should proceed to make the Four Universal Vows and work to cultivate and fulfill them. There are limitless sentient beings tormented by the sufferings of birth and death. How can we not resolve to rescue these beings and guide them to the other shore? How can we not resolve to help them unlock those shackles, eradicate afflictions and the accumulation of karma, and free themselves to experience complete liberation from all suffering?

Of course, it is not easy to eliminate the causes of suffering. To do so, we need to rely not only on the power of our vows, but also on the power of the great vows of highly cultivated masters, bodhisattvas, and Buddhas to guide us in our practice. The power of vows is emphasized in the *Great Perfection of Wisdom Treatise*, "When generating merits without making vows, there is no set aim to direct the result to, for vows serve as the guide to direct one toward realizing accomplishments. This is like shaping gold pieces. The process is dependent upon the goldsmith, for gold does not have a predetermined shape." The treatise further states, "Adorning the Buddha land is a great undertaking, one difficult to achieve with the cultivation of virtues and merits alone. The power of vows is required to fully accomplish this. As an analogy, the power of an ox can pull a cart, but a driver is required for the cart to reach its destination."

Buddhist sutras provide numerous examples clearly documenting that without the power of vows, Buddhas could not have attained Buddhahood. For example, Amitabha Buddha made forty-eight great vows to accomplish his Western Pure Land, as stated in the *Infinite Life Sutra*. The *Mahayana Compassionate Flower Sutra* tells us that Sakyamuni Buddha made five hundred great vows to attain Buddhahood, while Maitreya Bodhisattva fulfilled ten great vows to be the next Buddha in our world (*Questions Asked by Maitreya Sutra*). And to eliminate the suffering of sentient beings, the Medicine Buddha made twelve great vows to accomplish the Land of Pure Crystal (*Medicine Buddha Sutra*). These examples further demonstrate that the vows made by the Buddhas and bodhisattvas abide within the paradigm of the Four Universal Vows.

The *Collection of Translated Terms* states that practicing Buddhism requires three states of mind: the mind of great wisdom, the mind of great compassion, and the mind of great vow. Aspiring to these three states of mind means to follow the Four Universal Vows, to aspire to the bodhi mind, to seek the attainment of Buddhahood, and to liberate all sentient beings. Let us look more closely at these vows.

1.   *Sentient beings are limitless; I vow to liberate them.*

As suggested by the Buddhist adage, "Teaching the Dharma is my duty, and benefiting sentient beings is my mission," we, as Buddhists, must not only seek personal liberation, but also assume the responsibility of propagating the Dharma to liberate other sentient beings. In order to practice the Mahayana path, we must make this vow.

However, while it is easy to make such a vow to ourselves, it is much more difficult to make such a vow before the Buddhas and other sentient beings. Liberating sentient beings necessitates more than providing them with food when they are hungry or medicine when they are sick. These superficial provisions will not enhance their wisdom, nor help them to escape from the cycle of birth and death.

The *Diamond Sutra* states, "...be they born of eggs, wombs, moisture, or transformation, or whether they have form, or no form, or whether they are able to perceive, or do not perceive, or are neither able to perceive nor not perceive, I cause them to enter nirvana without remainder, liberating them." Ultimately, the approach to liberate sentient beings is to teach them the Dharma so that they can be free from afflictions and awaken to the Way.

2. *Afflictions are endless; I vow to eradicate them.*

To practice Buddhism is to fight our afflictions. Once our afflictions have been conquered, our Buddha nature will appear, and we will have made progress toward Buddhahood. Yet if we cannot end our own afflictions, not only will we be unable to escape suffering, it will be impossible to liberate other sentient beings. Consequently, the first thing we must do in practicing Buddhism is to live well ourselves and accomplish the cessation of all afflictions.

Afflictions can hurt us and prevent us from experiencing peace. For example, greed causes us to strive in harmful ways, resulting in suffering. Anger agitates us so that we cannot find serenity. Ignorance and wrong views cover our wisdom and prevent us from walking the right path. We must vow to eradicate all afflictions and diligently practice the threefold trainings of morality, meditative concentration, and wisdom that will enable us to achieve liberation and live with joy. The sutras describe a hierarchy of eighty-four thousand afflictions. Without the support of great vows, we could easily lose the whole battle and be claimed by the sea of our afflictions forever. Would this not be regrettable?

3. *Teachings are infinite; I vow to learn them.*

Generally, if we want to live a worry-free life, it is necessary to acquire many skills and forms of knowledge. To liberate sentient beings, not only do we need to learn Buddhism, but also all forms of knowledge open to us. To truly learn infinite teachings, we need to obtain worldly knowledge, the Buddha's teachings, and all manner of abilities. Just as the ocean accepts the current from the tiniest stream, so, too, should Buddhists learn all teachings to liberate all sentient beings.

The *Flower Adornment Sutra* actively encourages bodhisattvas to study and learn extensively, including the *Tripitaka* and the three-fold trainings, as well as the many teachings and methods of the numerous Buddhist schools. We must strive to learn them all!

4. *Buddhahood is supreme; I vow to attain it.*

Becoming a Buddha requires undergoing many hardships over long periods of time. Still, we should strive to follow in the footsteps of the sages and attempt to reach their level. By making this vow we not only pledge to attain Buddhahood for ourselves, but also for all sentient beings. This is the vow's true meaning.

In reality, the Buddha's attainment of Buddhahood was not merely the result of his birth in the human world, his renunciation, and his practice of asceticism. It also required his subjugation of maras, which include both the external temptations of sounds, senses, forms, and material gains, as well as the internal forces of greed, anger, and ignorance. As we cultivate through the many cycles of birth and death, there may be times when we become intimidated, lose our initial resolve, and are overrun by maras. However, the difficulty of the endeavor makes Buddhahood even more valuable.

In short, after understanding the Four Noble Truths, we need to emulate the bodhisattvas and learn all of the teachings. Then we need to apply these fundamental teachings in our lives, including the Four Noble Truths, the four means of embracing, and the six perfections, in order to fulfill the Four Universal Vows of the bodhi-sattva path. The *Inspiration for the Bodhicitta Pledge* states, "The most important entrance to the path is determination. Cultivation is a pressing matter, but one must first make vows. Once vows have been made, sentient beings can be liberated. With determination, Buddhahood can be attained."

From Truth to Vows—The Path of Freedom

It is important to realize that the Four Universal Vows of Mahayana Buddhism are deep commitments and great promises that developed from the Four Noble Truths. They share the same essence. And such a parallel grants us a greater understanding of the concept of practice across Buddhist schools.

The *Great Text of Stopping [Delusion] and Seeing [Truth]* by Master Zhiyi describes the Four Universal Vows as being borne from the wisdom of the Four Noble Truths. He continues, explaining that Mahayana bodhisattvas, whose bodhi mind has arisen as a result of learning and practicing the Four Noble Truths, need to fulfill the bodhisattva path and expound the true nature of the Four Universal Vows. Indeed, Buddhist scriptures, such as the *Agama Sutra*, are rich with teachings of the Buddha that reflect the importance of spreading the Dharma for the benefit all sentient beings.

This is the basis for the deep and profound relationship between the Four Noble Truths and the Four Universal Vows. As mentioned earlier, after understanding the Four Noble Truths we need the power of the great vows to guide us toward liberation from suffering. As sentient beings who are mired in the difficulties and torments of life, we struggle to cross to the other shore of enlightenment, but we cannot even find the ferry. Therefore, we need the sages and wise teachers who pilot the ships of great vows.

The four great bodhisattvas, Avalokitesvara, Manjusri, Ksitigarbha, and Samantabhadra, are the embodiment and personification of the Four Universal Vows. Their combined achievement of merits and virtues lead to the realization of the ideal world of perfect enlightenment and contemplation. Through the spirit of their great vows, they encourage our own footsteps on the path. We can begin use our blossoming understanding of the Four Noble Truths to find our own spiritual voice, our own strength of commitment, and our own expression of compassion and loving-kindness.

The Essence of Learning and Insight

Though the Buddha often spoke on the same truth, he applied different teaching approaches according to the situation, location, and his audiences' knowledge and potential. This demonstrates the Buddha's expertise or skillful means in teaching the Dharma. This is why the Buddha would, at times, teach existence and at other times, emptiness; at times, teach nature and at other times, form; at times teach entities and at other times, functionality.

These examples express two related points to understand and consider when learning the Dharma. First of all, just as the Buddha recognized the varying needs of his audiences, we too, can use skillful means to aid our own understanding of the teachings as well as to assist others. We can listen to wise teachers, study sutras and commentaries, and attend Dharma functions, all the while building skillful means into our own way of communicating. Secondly, the Buddha specifically established the four reliances as the basis of learning the Dharma, and to help us recognize the true teachings.

1. *Rely on the Dharma, not on individual teachers.* People espouse varied beliefs and perceptions and are subject to impermanence, but the Dharma never changes.

2. *Rely on the meaning, not on the words.* If we are too attached to words, we end up with a superficial understanding and will not comprehend something's real meaning.

3. *Rely on wisdom, not on knowledge.* Wisdom is the truth that already lies within us. Knowledge comes from our experiences in the outside world and constantly shifts. When we use wisdom as a mirror to look at phenomena, it will reflect things as they really are.

4. *Rely on the ultimate truth, not the relative truth.* This means that we rely on the definitive meaning and not on the various methods of teaching. We should rely on our mind of wisdom which comes from our own Buddha nature rather than our ordinary, judgmental mind.

Our learning and cultivation of the Dharma should be based on the fundamental teachings of the Four Noble Truths, the three Dharma seals, and the twelve links of dependent origination, before moving on to the Four Universal Vows. These skillful teachings give substance and direction to our vows, and with time and proper progression we can come to understand them all. The Dharma is adaptable, all-encompassing, and capable of perfect integration in order to meet the needs of all who choose to enter the path.

Therefore, Buddhahood is possible to achieve! After gaining insight into the Four Noble Truths and the Four Universal Vows, we are able to give rise to the bodhi mind, make vows in accordance with the Dharma, practice diligently without indolence, and accumulate merits, virtues, and good conditions. Then, Buddhahood will be within our reach.

Chapter Two

On Cause, Condition and Effect: The Way of Dependent Origination

While sitting under the bodhi tree, the Buddha gazed up at the stars and attained awakening. The truth that he awakened to was the universal truth of dependent origination, one of the central teachings of Buddhism. Dependent origination is also the most significant characteristic that distinguishes Buddhism from other philosophies and religions.

What is dependent origination? Dependent origination means that all phenomena arise and cease due to causes and conditions. The *Commentary on the Surangama Sutra* states, "All teachings, from the simplest to the most profound say that phenomena do not exist outside of causes and conditions."

But the human perspective is narrow and confined, and can hinder us from looking at the world with wisdom. Worldly happiness and suffering do not have an absolute existence of their own. They arise because of the discriminations we make through our perceptions and thinking. To understand and accept the Buddhist teachings, we need to change our perspectives. We must go beyond the superficial of name and form to see things as they really are, illuminate our wisdom, and sow the seeds of awakening. Only then will the water of the Dharma flow into the spiritual fields of our minds.

Dependent Origination and Causes and Conditions

Everything in the world comes into being because of causes and conditions. Without this principle, no phenomena would arise, and nothing could exist. Explained in this way, the truth of dependent origination may appear simplistic or trivial, yet it has far-reaching consequences. It means that nothing in the universe has an independent existence of its own. It also means that there is no absolute phenomenon anywhere in the universe. There is no "self" that exists separately from others. Therefore, since all phenomena are interdependent, if the causes and conditions that produce or sustain a phenomenon are removed, that phenomenon will cease to exist.

This is the teaching of the Buddha. But what are causes and conditions? Where do they come from? Actually, causes and conditions themselves are phenomena, and they arise from other causes and conditions. Some phenomena are labeled "causes" and others are labeled "conditions" to help us understand how phenomena arise and cease. But these terms only take on meaning in relationship to one another. What is considered a "cause" in one instance may be considered a "condition" in another, depending on the angle from which phenomena are observed.

Causes and conditions comprise the two basic factors that produce or underlie each and every phenomenon in the universe. The more powerful, primary factors that lead to the arising of a phenomenon are called "causes," while the secondary, supporting factors are called "conditions." For example, a seed that is planted in the soil needs water, fertilizer, air, and sunlight to grow. The seed is the cause. The soil, water, fertilizer, air, and sunlight are the conditions. Only when all of the right causes and conditions are present will there be the result of a healthy plant. Without a cause, there could be no effect. With a cause but no conditions, there would also be no effect. Causes and the conditions must exist together, to produce an effect. The plant is in the seed and the seed is in the plant, arising in mutual dependence. Therefore, causes and effects can be said to co-arise, and all phenomena result from multiple causes and conditions.

Dependent origination is not something invented by the Buddha. It is a natural, universal principle underlying all phenomena in the universe. When the Buddha attained awakening, he realized this principle. After his awakening, he taught others what he had come to understand. The Buddha taught that if we learn to contemplate the concept of causes and conditions from the perspective of sentient beings trapped within the cycle of birth and death, we will see that our lives are not the creation of a deity that stands outside of the universe. Rather, our lives result from a complex interaction of causes and conditions.

Dependent Origination and Cause and Effect

The *Connected Discourses* say, "This exists, therefore, that exists. This arises, therefore, that arises. This is absent, therefore, that is absent. This is extinguished, therefore, that is extinguished." The "this" and "that" refer to cause and effect, and the quote implies that both coexist in a state of dynamic interaction. Without one, the other could not be. Just as the words "cause" and "condition" are relative terms, so are the words "cause" and "effect." The Buddha used these terms to help us understand some of the general features of this web of phenomena. It is important for each one of us to try to comprehend this universe because this is where we live. We are a part of it, and what we think about it has great influence both on ourselves and on other sentient beings.

Cause and effect are related, but the roles they play are not absolute. Causes produce effects, but those effects in turn produce other effects, and in doing so, become causes. Therefore, causes and effects are really interlocking parts of an endless chain of events. Present causes contain many previous causes. Following this logic, we can see that there is no first cause and no last effect. Likewise, after the present effect more effects will follow. Because of this universal, there is no ultimate end. Sometimes, it is hard for us to comprehend and accept that all our intentional behavior produces effects. Yet, we cannot hide from the consequences of our own actions. We might wait ten million years, but one day, when the conditions are right, the effects of our choices will manifest. In order to arrive at a better understanding of dependent origination, let us examine six of its key principles.

1. *Effects Arise from Causes*

Dependent origination first depends on the presence of a cause and then on the right conditions before the effect can manifest. If there is no cause, there can be no effect. If there is a cause, but conditions are not right, then there is also no effect. A cause phenomenon is a primary, direct requirement to produce an effect. A condition phenomenon is an external, indirect requirement to help a cause to produce an effect.

The earlier example of the seed provides insight into the nature of this principle in the physical world. But as all phenomena in the universe are governed by causes and conditions, dependent origination also applies to the behavior of sentient beings, our karma. For example, all human beings hold within them the seed, the necessary cause to become Buddhas. But if this seed is not nourished by good conditions such as studying the Dharma, upholding the precepts, and so forth, the effect of Buddhahood will not arise. Similarly, a person who carries a latent cause of anger might be able to control this anger for years. However if conditions are right, the person may suddenly explode, seemingly without reason.

Sometimes it is hard for us to comprehend and accept that all our intentional behavior produces years, but one day when the conditions are right the effects of our choices will manifest. The importance of this insight cannot be understated. Yet, dependent origination also reflects an immense, positive human potential. Our present is in our hands. Our future is in our hands. Our choices determine the nature of our present life and the direction of our future lives for ourselves and for those around us. We need only take the responsibility.

2. Phenomena Are Temporary

From the above principle, we know that all phenomena arise due to the interaction between causes and conditions. In this same way, all phenomena also cease due to causes and conditions. If we are mindful, we can begin to realize and observe that all phenomena merely appear temporarily and have no substantial existence of their own. Without a substantial existence, phenomena appear when the right conditions arise, and disappear when the right conditions cease.

Let us return to the example involving anger. If through our practice we become mindful of our behavior, we can avoid planting that seed of anger, without which there will be no effect of a later outburst. Similarly, if we do plant the seed of anger through our decisions, but follow with acts of repentance and good works, we could postpone or lessen a later effect. In other words, phenomena change precisely because causes and conditions change.

3. Events Depend on Corresponding Truths

Phenomena arise due to causes and conditions, but they also do so in a correspondent manner. For example, if you plant a pumpkin seed, you will not reap a tomato. The causes of a certain type produce effects that are consistent with that type. In the same way, our positive actions bring positive effects, while negative actions result in unhappy results. This is a universal truth; there is no event that occurs outside of this principle.

Additionally, the workings of cause and effect span the past, present, and future. Even though we cannot see into the past or future, we can see what happens in the present. The sutras say, "If we want to know the causes we have planted in our past lives, our experiences in this life are the effects. If we want to know what our circumstances will be in the next life, just look at the causes we are planting in this life."

4. Many Come from One

To most people, one is one, and many is many. But from a Buddhist perspective, one cause can lead to many effects and multiple causes can result in a single, large effect. Often, people do not look at the world in this way and do not realize the potential that lies within things, especially the potential within the human mind. A seed may grow into a tree that yields much fruit, so we can say that abundance can come from a single seed. Likewise, a single, small act of kindness may create many ripples that change the world for the better, while one, small act of cruelty could cause numerous, far-reaching, destructive results.

5. Existence Relies on Emptiness

The word "emptiness" is an English translation of the Sanskrit word *sunyata*. In Buddhist terminology, emptiness is used to describe the ultimate nature of reality that nothing has an independent self. However, emptiness is often misinterpreted and instead seen as a justification for pessimism and seclusion. When understood correctly, we will see that emptiness embraces the boundless universe and gives rise to all existence. Emptiness is not negation; it is relieving the mind of the notions of relativity, duality, and distinction. The *Middle Way Treatise* says, "Because there is emptiness, all phenomena exist. Without emptiness, all phenomena could not be."

A common example used to explain this point is that of the wooden table. A table comes from a tree, and the tree depends on the conditions of soil, water, and sunshine to grow. Even though a table appears to have some substantial existence, it actually relies on numerous conditions coming together so that it may arise temporarily. Aside from the external conditions resulting in the tree's existence, someone had to cut the tree, move it, make the table, and put it in your room. As soon as we begin to investigate the causes and the conditions on which the table depends for its existence, we find that, ultimately, there is no "table nature." Rather, what we think of as a table is actually an endlessly complex web of interconnectedness, impermanence, and change. If even one element is removed from that web, there might not be a table at all.

None of this says that the table does not exist. It means that the nature of a table is empty of an independent existence. If the nature of phenomena were not empty, phenomena would have no value. This is what emptiness does, it gives things value and purpose. The value and function of a table belong to conventional reality. The emptiness of the table belongs to ultimate reality.

Therefore, emptiness does not mean pessimism and nihilism. Rather, emptiness is creative and constructive. By understanding emptiness we can let go of the attachments that we cling to, and see the world from a different perspective. When we have experienced and directly realized emptiness, we will be in harmony with the entire universe.

6.   *A Buddha Comes from a Human Being*

When Sakyamuni Buddha awakened, he said, "All sentient beings have the Tathagata's wisdom and virtue, but they fail to realize it because they cling to deluded thoughts and attachments." The Buddha said time and again that all of us have Buddha nature and that anyone who works long and hard enough at purifying his or her mind will eventually become a Buddha as well. Our attachments are like dark clouds that conceal the brightness of the moon or like mud that obscures a pond's clear water.

In our study of Buddhism, we must understand the cycle of birth and death and the truth that, "This is absent, therefore, that is absent. This ceases, therefore, that ceases." With this insight, we can put an end to our ignorance and reveal our Buddha nature. In this way we can attain the state of non-duality, the state without the limitations of space and time or birth and death. This is awakening.

There is a saying in Buddhism, "A Buddha is an awakened sentient being. Sentient beings are merely unawakened Buddhas." The *Principles of the Six Perfections Sutra* says, "All sentient beings enter the wisdom of the Buddha by purifying the mind. The nature of a Buddha is no different from that of any other sentient being."

Dependent Origination and Human Life

Dependent origination shows us the relationship between the arising, abiding, changing, and ceasing of phenomena, as well as the origin of human suffering. Whenever we ignore this reality and attach to the delusion of permanence, we bring suffering upon ourselves. In contrast, when we are mindful of the forces that affect the phenomenal world, we prepare ourselves to cope with them in a positive and productive manner. When we understand that many are born from one and that all conditions are caused, we will realize how to bring about good conditions in our own lives and in the world.

A true understanding of dependent origination will also bring us joy, for it teaches us that the future lies in our own hands. Future conditions and effects depend on causal seeds that we plant today. Liberation is achieved through practicing and understanding this truth for the benefit of ourselves and all sentient beings. Therefore, dependent origination strengthens the mind because it teaches us how to determine what is most valuable in life and how to turn negative circumstances into positive ones.

As dependent origination demonstrates that nothing in the world is permanent, we can learn to understand that all phenomena are conditioned by other phenomena and that all of them rely on emptiness. Nothing has a substantial existence, including us. We, too, are empty. Clear understanding of this truth leads to a reality that lies beyond greed, anger, ignorance, attachment, suffering, and all delusions of duality. If we can channel the energy we expend perpetrating harm into performing wholesome actions, if we can maintain resolve when problems arise, and if we can do what is right and not what is easy, we will one day reap the fruits of our labor.

Consistent contemplation of dependent origination inspires us to be grateful for the things we have and for the world in which we live. We can learn how to flow with life in a way that benefits both ourselves and others. Dependent origination gives us hope as it shows us how to understand the deepest meaning of life. The *Rice Stalk Sutra* says, "To see dependent origination is to see the Dharma. To see the Dharma is to see the Buddha."

Chapter Three

On Knowledge: The Way of Study

S tudy and scholarship function to increase human knowledge and bring wisdom as well as to improve disposition, perfect character, and alter temperament. This is why it is said that "by knowing the classics one glorifies oneself." And this is why since ancient times, wise people have encouraged everyone to study. Today, the wealth of Buddhist literature and scriptures continues this role, serving to deepen our insight and positively inform our personal practice, while generating the necessary causes and conditions to compassionately share the Buddha's teachings.

Buddhism is a religion of wisdom and faith. Its aim is to enlighten sentient beings as well as to eliminate their afflictions and sufferings. This is why Buddhism places emphasis on the life of a scholar, encouraging all Buddhists to read the scriptures and listen to the Dharma. In other words, to reap the benefits of such practice requires a lifetime; thus study and practice become synonymous with life. Numerous sutras echo this timeless truth. For example, the *Father and Son Sutra* teaches, "If sentient beings hear the Buddha's words, their hearts will give rise to a pure faith and a resolve to attain liberation; by single-mindedly practicing the wonderful Way, they will attain perfect wisdom, transcending the sea of *samsara*." And the *Flower Adornment Sutra* affirms, "of all offerings, an offering of the Dharma is best."

Buddhism has always emphasized study to foster wisdom. In ancient times, temples and monasteries served as schools where monastics could study and practice the Way and were, in fact, called "the venue for selecting the Buddha." These early educational practices placed a premium on the transmission of written wisdom, generating a rich tradition of transmittable knowledge. The ten Dharma practices of the *Lotus Sutra*, for example, include the benefits of writing, speaking, reading, and printing the sutras. The *Amitabha Sutra* states that at every hour of every day, beings who reside in the Pure Land reflect upon the Buddha, the Dharma, and the Sangha. The "Entering the Dharma Realm" chapter of the *Flower Adornment Sutra* tells how young Sudhana sets his mind on seeking the Dharma and goes through the arduous process of traveling to visit fifty-three good Dharma friends in the search for knowledge. This is similar to the study abroad programs of today and serves as a model for today's youth as they venture forth to study.

Traditionally, almost every temple contained a building in which the scriptures were kept. In addition to the ten thousand words chanted daily, there exists the legacy of handwritten, pattra-leaf sutras as well as those carved in stone. Then there are the examples of Bhiksuni Fazhen, who lost an arm printing sutras during the Yuan dynasty; and Master Xuanzhuang, who collected sutras in India and the western regions of China and Dharmodgata, and spread the Dharma to the East. They sought out and propagated the Dharma without thinking of themselves. Had they not studied, would this have been possible? Without scholarly dedication, would we possess the Buddhist canon today?

Master Zhuhong of the Ming dynasty advocated, "Everyone in this world has something they like, and this they pursue all the days of their lives. The best are those who like to study; they benefit from reading. Even better is studying the Buddhist sutras and purifying one's mind. The purity of the mind is the greatest to nurture for worldly and transcendental living. Gradually entering this perfect state is like eating sugarcane." From these examples, it is clear that the moral exemplars of antiquity emphasized study, especially the earnest study of the written scriptures.

From ancient times, all monastics have been well versed in the scriptures. Naturally, most of them were intellectuals and had close connections with the scholarly class. Yet in traditional China, male and female villagers who could not recite the Confucian classics could recite Buddhist texts such as the *Great Compassion Dharani*, the *Diamond Sutra*, and the *Amitabha Sutra*. Clearly, the Buddhist advocacy for education has greatly impacted Chinese society. As a developing trend, many elders at the end of the Qing dynasty and the beginning of the Republic of China established both monastic and secular schools. Master Taixu, in particular, founded many Buddhist academies, paving the way for an increase in formal educational opportunities for the laity.

According to the *Contemplation of the Mind Sutra*, "First become friends with good Dharma friends; second, listen to the true Dharma; third, contemplate the truth; and fourth practice the Way." The *Vigilance for All Monastics* asserts, "Nothing is possible without study. Nothing can be learned without humbling oneself; the Dharma cannot be held without a teacher; nothing will be remembered without practice and recitation." Buddhism stresses both the transmission of knowledge and the cultivation of wisdom. However, Buddhist education differs from ordinary education that seeks to develop skills to earn a living or a diploma to obtain a good job.

Buddhist education includes compassion, a shouldering of the great burden to benefit oneself and others.

Today, there are Sunday schools and summer camps for children as well as youth groups and college groups for young people. Practice and study groups abound for adult devotees, along with Buddhist institutes and graduate schools for professionals. As a specific example, these opportunities along with primary schools, secondary schools, and universities established worldwide by the Fo Guang Shan Buddhist Order receive the support of thousands of devotees, clearly demonstrating the importance of education and scholarship within the Buddhist community.

Currently, higher Buddhist education often falls into the two categories of temple administration and theoretical research, with special emphasis on education for life and thought. Life education includes training in walking, dwelling, sitting, resting, communication and other behavioral skills. In a complementary capacity, thought education involves the personal development of the four objects of unfailing faith:

1. Faith in the Triple Gem;
2. Loyalty for the temple;
3. Loving-kindness for all sentient beings; and
4. Firmness in upholding the precepts.

And, whether formal or informal, study must be self-motivated and spontaneous. Individual initiative is the key.

While its importance cannot be overstated as a foundation for understanding the Buddha's teachings, Buddhism does not rest solely on the academic exploration of knowledge, theory, and ethics, but equally emphasizes the necessity practice and cultivation in daily life. The *Lankavatara Sutra* states, "If one hears the Dharma but fails to practice it, it is the same as never having heard it." Thus, the study and practice of Buddhism are not limited to temples, monasteries, and educational institutions. A day's practice involves interacting with others by following the example of the Buddha and the bodhisattvas, and acting with compassion as related by the Dharma.

A day's practice for a Buddhist looks something like this: from rising in the morning until retiring in the evening, we interact with others with speech, silence, action, and non-action. We should use words of compassion to reply to others, look at others with compassionate eyes, present a compassionate appearance to others, assist others with hands of compassion, and bless others with a compassionate heart. Only when life is imbued with the Dharma can it be called practice. Theory translates into life strategies; sutras become our guides. By following the example of the Buddha and the bodhisattvas, one acts with compassion toward others, living the Dharma.

Additionally, we can use our personal time to focus on studies and to persevere. For example, if space permits we can create a Buddhist shrine in our home. Each morning we can offer flowers or water, light a stick of incense and pray, recite the scriptures, or sit in meditation for five minutes before a Buddha's or a bodhisattva's image. At night before going to bed, we can calm our mind before the image of the Buddha or recite Buddhist prayers while contemplating personal achievements and errors. Once or twice each week we can attend religious practice at a temple, partaking in the joys of religion, cleansing ourselves of greed, anger, and afflictions while developing spiritual riches. Each day before a meal, we should join our palms and recite the four offerings, the BLIA Verse, or the five meal contemplations to cultivate a spiritual sense of thankfulness and compassion.

In all of these ways, Buddhist study informs practice and practice informs our interactions with the world. And whether private or public, informal or formal, practice includes going to temples, acquiring good knowledge, and seeking the Dharma for the benefit of all. This is the practice advocated by Humanistic Buddhism.

Chapter Four

On Religion: The Way of Faith

Humans are spiritual beings, and religion is like the sunlight and water without which we could not live. Even in our most remote past, human beings professed a faith in and a respect for the forces of nature. What followed was the evolution of increasingly sophisticated, multifaceted, political and religious systems which impacted the human rights of their day while projecting the potential for the rights of all living things into the future. Therefore, history shows us that people, ancient and modern, have always sought not only a satisfying material life but also a spiritual life of faith.

Broadly defined, faith refers to belief, trust, or confidence in something, though not necessarily involving religion. For example, some people have faith in a particular idea or theory, some people have faith in a particular "ism," while others worship a person to the extent that their activities become a faith. Yet, once questions of life and death are posed, religious faith often takes on importance.

Faith in a religion requires careful choices, for to fall into beliefs that cause harm to ourselves or others is no different than drinking poison. Once the poison takes hold, our life and the lives of those around us are at risk. It is, therefore, better to have no beliefs at all than to espouse harmful beliefs. Additionally, nonreligious super-stition is superior to holding no beliefs because, at the very least, superstition involves the concepts of good and evil and cause and effect. The tendency is to do good and to shun evil. A person with-out faith or beliefs is like a person who refuses to open their eyes to reality. Never will they create the causes and conditions necessary to understand the world without the blinders of ignorance.

The ultimate form of religious faith is, of course, a correct or right-minded faith, one that is ethical, virtuous and subscribes to the prin-ciple of causing no harm. This kind of faith possesses certain char-acteristics. Using Buddhism as an example, we can understand that:

1. *A faith must have an historical basis*: In the case of Bud-dhism, there are historical records of Sakyamuni Bud-dha's parents, his clan, his place and date of birth, and his process of leaving home, cultivation, and enlightenment.

2. *A faith must be widely acknowledged*: Buddhism ranks within the top five of the world's largest religions.

3. *There must an emphasis on human dignity, morality, and perfection*: The Buddha, for example, possesses the three complete virtues of wisdom, freedom from ignorance, and universal grace. He is the perfectly enlightened prac-titioner of merit.

4. *The power of faith must be awe-inspiring and complete*: Buddhism's three Dharma seals, the Four Noble Truths, the Noble Eightfold Path, as well as the laws of cause and effect, karma, and dependent origination represent truths founded upon the world's natural laws. These truths can help guide us toward enlightenment and the insight to forsake suffering for happiness.

Faith is the ultimate goal. It can support us in life. Regardless of the religion in which we believe, a rational choice must be made based on whether or not its teachings correspond to the truth. This is to say that a religion must involve a faith that is universal, equal, real, and eternal. As one example, the Buddhist scriptures speak of the "four unattainables" of perpetual youth, no sickness, perennial life, and no death. This is a universal reality, as true in history as it is today, and as it will be in the future.

Buddhism is a religion that corresponds to this truth. But as in other religions, not all practitioners perceive it in the same way or possess the same level of faith. For example, some people believe in a person and not in the Dharma; some people believe in a temple but not in a religion; some people believe in a feeling and not in the Way, and some people believe in spirits but not in the Buddhas. There are even differences in faith within Buddhist teachings. For most people, wisdom is synonymous with correct views. For others, wisdom refers to dependent origination. For the bodhisattva, wisdom is emptiness. Only the Buddha is capable of true, complete awareness of wisdom. Wisdom is the realm of the Buddhas, the supreme Dharma realm.

In his career of teaching the Dharma to liberate sentient beings, the Buddha divided the Dharma into five methods of practice called the "five vehicles," based upon the spiritual capacities of his followers. Employing these five methods of practice can convey beings from the cycle of birth and death of this shore to the nirvana of the other shore. The five vehicles are the human vehicle, the heavenly vehicle, the sravaka vehicle, the pratyekabuddha vehicle, and the bodhisattva vehicle. In addition, you might recognize how these five vehicles illuminate underlying connections with other religious faiths, thereby demonstrating universal truths.

Buddhist practice for humans and heavenly beings focuses on improving the mind by acting virtuously, so that we might achieve happiness in our current life and the next. This is the aspect of the Dharma that is held in common with the whole world. Buddhist practice for srvakas and pratyekabuddhas emphasizes a detached mind for liberation and transcendence of the mundane world. The ultimate goal of these vehicles is the bliss of nirvana. The bodhisattva vehicle is founded upon developing bodhi mind, the mind that aspires to awakening, and wishes to benefit others and liberate the world. The ultimate goal of this practice is to cultivate the supreme happiness of wisdom and compassion and to liberate all sentient beings through the practice of the six perfections and all modes of liberation.

We can see that the teachings of Buddhism are profound and all encompassing, and it is in the details of our practice that we uncover the Way. For example, in addition to taking refuge in the Triple Gem advocated by Buddhism, we can pay respect to Buddhas and heavenly beings. But, taking refuge and the act of worship represent different aspects of Buddhist practice. Taking refuge involves vows of faith for a lifetime, while the act of worship is a moment of paying respect. Therefore, those of us who have taken refuge in the Triple Gem can pay respect to the Buddhist deities. But faith presupposes a single-minded, focused mind. Hence, we read in the "Universal Gate" chapter of the *Lotus Sutra*, "single-mindedly recite the bodhisattva's name" and "single-mindedly make offerings." In the *Amitabha Sutra* we read, "single-mindedly wish to be reborn in the Western Pure Land." These quotations stand as proof of the importance of a wholehearted sincerity of spirit. Therefore, as adherents of a particular religion must be loyal to their chosen faith. We must remain focused, for when our faith conflicts with our feelings, financial status, occupation, or future, we are better able to single-mindedly confront the tests.

It does not matter in what religion we believe. The most important endeavor is to uncover our original nature, a nature that embraces compassion and an understanding of dependent origination and the law of cause and effect. If we possess correct or right-minded faith not only will we have spiritual and mental support, we can also form good affinities with like-minded friends. As the *Buddhist Canon of the Theravada Tradition* asserts, "In a household that has faith, there are four types of morality: sincerity, truth, firmness, and giving charity." With these four types of morality, "there will be no fear or anxieties with regard to the present or the future." If we harbor no fear or anxiety toward life and death, then from a Buddhist perspective, we already possess correct faith. Just as the *Diamond Sutra* notes, "If a person can produce even one thought of pure faith, that person will achieve complete and perfect enlightenment."

In conclusion, religious faith can inspire us with the courage and strength to face the future. It can provide us with the magnanimity to forgive the unfairness of life and, thereby, create an entirely new fate. The teachings of Buddhism, especially the Middle Way and dependent origination, the law of cause and effect, and nirvana can all help us to solve the riddle of life, revealing the original Buddha nature of all people. Thus, a belief in Buddhism involves a progression from beseeching, believing in, and worshiping the Buddha, to studying Buddhism and doing as the Buddha did to become a Buddha, which is the highest faith of all.

PART II

Living in the World

Use a kind, compassionate heart to
   care for all living beings;

use kind, compassionate eyes to
   look at all things;

use kind, compassionate words to
   rejoice in and praise others;

use kind, compassionate hands to
   do good deeds broadly.

— *Humble Table, Wise Fair*
Inspirtation

Chapter Five

On Emotions:
The Way of Love and Affection

In our complicated lives, many forms and types of relationships exist. There are friendships, family connections, teacher-student bonds, marriages, and relationships with and between monastics, to name a few. How we choose to develop, nurture, and manage these relationships determines our own joy and contentment, as well as that of our fellow human beings. How wonderful our lives become when we trust in the infinite and inherent capacity for connection that all beings share. Living with utmost ease and happiness and with the maximum ability to benefit others depends on our capacity and willingness.

As explained by the twelve links of dependent origination, life originates from love. On the level of human emotion, love and affection are its roots, alive with potential for the flowering of compassion or ill will depending upon the ways we choose to nourish these roots. Therefore, our existence plays out on a continuum of emotion. While some kinds of love are healthy and giving, others are unhealthy and become possessive.

Humans are emotionally conscious beings, referred to in Buddhist texts as "sentient beings." And as sentient beings, we navigate the emotionally charged seas of our lives in every moment. But, when we lack the insight to moderate our emotions, they can compel us to act in ways that we may later regret. Just reading the news, we notice the many suicides, acts of vengeance, and assaults resulting from emotions gone awry. Actually, love and hate are inseparable, one shadowing the other. Therefore, if we do not learn to love properly, if we do not expand our love to all, and if we do not elevate our love for a few to compassion for all, love can turn to hate.

The seeds of such volatile emotions lead to rebirth in samsara for numerous kalpas, an idea articulated by the *Illuminating Light Sutra.* "People are deluded on account of ordinary love and kindness and unable to rid themselves of passion and desire." Additionally, when love is parochial, finite in capacity, and limited in scope, it often becomes possessive and clinging. Thus, joy and sorrow build like water overflowing from a pool. While most of us know or long for the wonders of love, we may not understand why love can cause us so much pain. Therefore, let us examine three main situations in which love causes us problems:

1.   *When the Object of Our Love Is Inappropriate*

It is human nature to love someone with whom we feel a special affinity, but when the object of our emotions is inappropriate, heartache usually follows. When we love someone who is spoken for or is married to another, we are destined for trouble. It also takes two to love, and if the other person does not share these feelings, it is like banging our head against the wall. Therefore, depending on the object of our love, we should moderate our intensity accordingly or problems will arise.

2.   When Our Perspective of Love Is Inappropriate

One of the most common, though faulty, perspectives of love is to view it as some kind of trade. Some people believe that because of their personal wealth, they can buy love. Others dare not love those who are more affluent than themselves or would not consider falling in love with someone without first evaluating that person's looks, education, profession, or wealth. In these instances, love is viewed as a kind of transaction. But true love does not speak of requirements and prerequisites. True love is about giving.

3.   When the Manner in Which We Love Is Inappropriate

Some people love only themselves and have little regard for the feelings of others. In their continual pursuit of personal enjoyment, some even engage in violent encounters with their partners or extramarital affairs. Others let their emotions cloud their judgment, and they become partial to people they love and overly critical of those whom they dislike. Sometimes, love is, also, like a pair of rose-colored glasses, preventing us from seeing the true face of those we love or our own behavior.

Yes, these examples demonstrate that we can be misled by strong emotions. But love can also improve people, as illustrated in two examples from the *Lankavatara Sutra*. When the Buddha was in the world, Matangi was enamored of one of his disciples, the honorable Ananda. However, thanks to the skillful teaching of the Buddha, she realized that ordinary love is the root of suffering. Similarly, when Lotus Blossom Girl was in the world of human feelings, she was injured and sought revenge by toying with love. Later, under the tutelage of Maudgalyayana, she finally understood that inappropriate love is also the origin of suffering and was reformed.

The *Commentary of the Main Mahayana Doctrines* tells us that, "All sentient beings will be attached to love, and by reason of love commit wrongdoings and fall into evil. But if sentient beings can give rise to compassion and not be attached to love, they will be born in the upper realms by not creating unwholesome causes." Buddhism does not reject feelings. Rather it advocates that, as with Matangi and Utpalavarna, feelings can be imbued with compassion, purified by reason, circumscribed by etiquette, and guided by wisdom. Buddhism encourages love and intimacy between husband and wife, respect and forgiveness between parents and children, and care and cooperation among friends and colleagues. When we love properly, love brings out the best in each of us.

The Buddha's propagation of the Dharma to help others is love; his teachings and instructions for happiness are all love. Avalokitesvara Bodhisattva's great compassion, loving-kindness, and rescuing people from hardships and difficulty, are also love. Love helps us, gives us respect and freedom, and makes life easier. Love is beauty, goodness, and truth. Love is pure.

The bodhisattva cares about all sentient beings without distinction. For this reason, we should learn from the Buddhas and bodhisattvas to broaden and free love from its narrowest focus of loving ourselves and our family to loving everyone in our society, our country, and throughout the world. A possessive love can mature into one of giving, and finally into the enlightened love that the Buddhas and bodhisattvas have for us. And true love means helping and blessing the beloved. Through compassion we must expand the scope of love, purifying it through wisdom, respecting all that we love, and making sacrifices to fulfill our love. If there can be love and closeness among all people, how harmonious the world and universe would be!

Love guides ethics and provides order. It is love that binds people together and provides stability to the relationships between father and mother, husband and wife, sons and daughters, and friends. With love there is strength; with love there is hope. Buddhism will not deny or object to love as long as it is in accord with the law, morality, and the laws of human ethics. This is especially true of Humanistic Buddhism, which advocates the Middle Way. Life stems from love, and we must add dignity and beauty to it with pure, true, and compassionate love.

In this way, the Buddha teaches us to use compassion to channel our emotions and wisdom to guide the unbridled forces of our emotions. While we often think of the Buddha as the fully enlightened one, we should not forget that he was also a most affectionate and loving human being. The Buddha certainly experienced emotions, but he did so without attachment to them. In other words, they had no power to overwhelm him or control his behavior.

With the insight of these teachings, consider the following four guidelines:

1. *Love wisely.* We should use our wisdom to purify our love.
2. *Love compassionately.* We should use our compassion to manifest our love.
3. *Love in accordance with the Dharma.* We should use the Dharma to guide our love.
4. *Love morally.* We should use morals and ethics to direct our love.

Love is like water. On the one hand, it can nurture our lives; on the other hand, it can drown us. If we do not know how to love properly, love can bring us many problems and ruin our lives. If we are ordinary in how we love and selective about who we love, love's vast dimensions will be hardly actualized. But when we begin to wear the Buddha's teachings, and when we offer our love and affection to all beings, our lives will become more peaceful, more rewarding, and more joyful!

Chapter Six

On Loving-Kindness and Compassion: The Way of Becoming a Bodhisattva

Often, when discussing bodhisattvas, we immediately think of the clay or wooden statues that we pay our respects to in temples, or the images we find in paintings or sculptures. Most people think of them as deities who have innumerable supernatural powers and are mystical beyond the capacity of human understanding. We think of bodhisattvas as beings who have the Midas touch, are able to command the wind and rain, and can bestow wealth upon us.

Actually, bodhisattvas are not deities who sit above us or lie outside our comprehension. Their presence is not distant at all, but right here in our midst. Bodhisattvas are not idols to whom we make offerings. A true bodhisattva resides among us, for a true bodhisattva is someone rich in compassion and most earnest in liberating all sentient beings within the six realms of existence. This is their great vow. A bodhisattva is a consummate practitioner who is walking on the path toward Buddhahood, benefiting all sentient beings as well as themselves. We can all become bodhisattvas, and to fully realize the bodhisattva way of life is the goal of Humanistic Buddhism.

The word *bodhisattva* derives from two Sanskrit words, *bodhi* meaning to awaken and *sattva* referring to sentient beings. Therefore, a bodhisattva is a sentient being who is seeking awakening. Bodhisattvas are beings who perfect the practice benefiting both themselves and others in their pursuit of awakening. When we make a Mahayana vow to seek the Way, helping and liberating sentient beings becomes our primary responsibility.

The Mind of a Bodhisattva

The mind of the bodhisattva requires the mind of bodhi, the mind of great compassion, and the mind of skillful means. Master Taixu said that the mind of bodhi is the cause, the mind of great compassion is the root, and the mind of skillful means is the ultimate truth. In Mahayana Buddhism, when practitioners are on the bodhisattva path, they must cultivate this kind of mind. The bodhi mind, therefore, is the mind that vows to liberate sentient beings and the mind that seeks the attainment of Buddhahood. Yet, the Way to Buddhahood requires countless kalpas of cultivation before it can be attained. If we do not give rise to the supreme bodhi mind, how can we bear such long-term challenges?

The sutras say that if one more person in the world initiates the bodhi mind, there will be one more seed of enlightenment. Practicing Buddhism without giving rise to the bodhi mind is like tilling the land without sowing seeds. If we do not sow any seeds, how can we have a harvest in the future? The bodhi mind is one that makes the great vow. To initiate the bodhi mind is to make the Four Universal Vows:

1. Sentient beings are limitless; I vow to liberate them.
2. Afflictions are endless; I vow to eradicate them.
3. Teachings are infinite; I vow to learn them.
4. Buddhahood is supreme; I vow to attain it.

Great compassion and loving-kindness are the qualities of mind that wish to liberate sentient beings. When a bodhisattva wishes to come to their aid, they must do so with a mind imbued with great loving-kindness and great compassion. A bodhisattva uses their great loving-kindness to bring others joy, and great compassion to remove their suffering. They treat the suffering and happiness of all sentient beings as their own, seeking nothing in return, and viewing helping others as their responsibility. Therefore, a bodhisattva is one who wishes to shoulder the burden of sentient beings, rather than pursuing peace and happiness for themselves. This is truly great compassion.

The mind of skillful means is the mind of practicing the four means of embracing: giving, kind words, altruism, and empathy. As sentient beings have varying needs and capacities to understand the Dharma, so bodhisattvas must wisely apply skillful means to liberate them. Having observed these differences, the Buddha imparted 84,000 teachings, which became his skillful means. A bodhisattva also applies the four means of embracing so that sentient beings can give rise to the ultimate, great happiness.

The Characteristics of a Bodhisattva

The bodhisattva's most unique characteristics are compassion and loving-kindness. Whenever bodhisattvas see sentient beings suffering, great compassion arises from deep within them, and they make a great vow to liberate them from their suffering. Therefore, compassion is the force that moves bodhisattvas to practice the Buddha Way of benefiting self and others.

The loving-kindness that bodhisattvas have for sentient beings is like the love that parents have for their children. To fulfill their needs, they would be willing to sacrifice their own lives. A bodhisattva's great loving-kindness and compassion extends to all sentient beings just as the sun shines on every corner of the earth. And they use their loving-kindness and compassion as a foundation to apply wisdom to liberate sentient beings according to their individual needs.

One of the greatest bodhisattvas is Avalokitesvara Bodhisattva, who is known as the Bodhisattva of Compassion. With his incomparable compassion, he made twelve great vows to liberate all sentient beings. The name of Avalokitesvara Bodhisattva is translated into Chinese as *guanshiyin*, which means observing the sounds of the world. At any time and in any place, he is able to observe the cries of sentient beings seeking assistance and apply his supernatural powers and skillful means to manifest before them. As long as there are sentient beings who cry out for help, Avalokitesvara Bodhisattva will appear and respond. In accordance with their various needs, he appears in any of his thirty-two manifestations whenever he is needed to relieve suffering and distress.

The Practice of the Bodhisattva Path

Buddhism is a religion that emphasizes practice, but it is also a philosophy with ethical characteristics. The Buddhist sutras contain many profound doctrines on truth and the universe, and in this sense Buddhism can be considered a philosophy. However, as Buddhism places great emphasis on the application of morality and ethics to life, so it can also be classified as a religion. In fact, the Buddha himself was regarded as a moral role model. After the Buddha attained awakening, he repeatedly taught that we should, "Do nothing that is unwholesome, do all that is wholesome, and purify the mind," with the hope that all sentient beings could purify themselves through moral conduct.

Practicing the bodhisattva path is just like any other kind of learning; we must go step by step. From the state of an ordinary person who has afflictions to the state of the bodhisattva who has cut off all defilements, there are definite states of cultivation. In order to progress through these stages and become a sage, a bodhisattva must fulfill the thirty-seven aspects of awakening, the four means of embracing, and the six perfections.

The thirty-seven aspects of awakening include the four bases of mindfulness, the four right efforts, the four bases of spiritual power, the five faculties, the five strengths, the seven factors of awakening and the Noble Eightfold Path. These methods are the resources that can help us cut off unwholesome deeds, develop wholesome conduct, eliminate ignorance, and enter the path of awakening. For these reasons, the practitioners on the bodhisattva path should diligently cultivate these thirty-seven aspects of awakening.

However, the most important teaching for developing the bodhisattva path is that of the six perfections. Called the six *paramitas* in Sanskrit, *paramita* means leading to the other shore or having accomplished the goal of awakening. Therefore, the six perfections liberate us from delusion and lead us to awakening, liberate us from evil and lead us toward the right path, liberate us from suffering and grant us happiness. They liberate all sentient beings from the shore of afflictions and ferry them to the other shore of liberation. The six perfections are forms of practice that bodhisattvas must cultivate in order to become Buddhas:

1. *The perfection of giving* is the generous mind of giving charity without attachment to form. All gifts should be given without attachment to what is being given, or who is giving or receiving the gift.

2. *The perfection of morality* is the non-violating mind of respecting sentient beings. Observing the Buddhist precepts, acting in accordance with right Dharma, and practicing the path of benefiting sentient beings is the bodhisattva's path of morality.

3. *The perfection of patience* is the mind of equanimity that enables us to endure what is difficult to endure. To learn all teachings, we should practice patience by being tolerant in the face of persecution, accepting in the midst adversity, and sincere in contemplating all truths. When we practice in this way, without retreating in fear, we are following the bodhisattva's path of patience.

4. *The perfection of diligence* is the fearless mind that refrains from unwholesome deeds and practices wholesome deeds. Bodhisattvas do not fear obstacles, but diligently develop courage, diligently practice the Dharma, and diligently bring joy and benefit to others. They do not tire of teaching even the most obstinate of sentient beings and apply their efforts ceaselessly.

5. *The perfection of meditative concentration* means to not differentiate with the mind and to maintain right mindfulness. Bodhisattvas apply meditative concentration to settle themselves and others and to demonstrate right mindfulness to all sentient beings.

6. *The perfection of prajna-wisdom* is the mind of great wisdom that lies beyond the duality of emptiness and existence. Bodhisattvas skillfully apply their prajna-wisdom

to inspire sentient beings to do what is right and good,
and gradually liberate them from their suffering.

In a life of suffering, people depend on loving-kindness and compassion. Loving-kindness and compassion provide a ray of hope in life. Society is often ruthless, tyrannical, and disorderly. And today, more than ever, people must insist on the habits of being amiable and equitable toward one another. We must learn to put ourselves in the shoes of others and consider all sentient beings as we would ourselves. This will give rise to loving-kindness and compassion.

The six perfections of a bodhisattva are altruistic and profound. A true practitioner practices the six perfections and protects the Dharma, enabling it to spread throughout the universe. Such a person sincerely strives to create a bright future to benefit all. Yet if we want to awaken our true capacity for happiness, we must first take down the walls that separate us. In this way, we can begin to recognize, affirm and strengthen the interlocking web of human relationships in which we all exist.

Chapter Seven

On Ethics and Morality:
The Way of Cultivating Affinity

The high-tech, fast paced societies of today emphasize planning, organization, and management in every aspect, from businesses and careers to families and other human relationships. All require management. Ultimately people need to know how to manage themselves as individuals. And, what we generally refer to as morality is the conscious attempt by individuals to benefit society. Indeed, Buddhism is a religion that emphasizes and blends daily practice, with ethical considerations.

But just how does Buddhism inform our individual conduct? What are Buddhist ethics? What would be considered moral behavior from a Buddhist perspective? For the sake of clarity, let us look briefly at these concepts. In the context of formal guidelines, ethics broadly refers to the external principles and standards by which a society, a religion, a business or a cultural group operates. In contrast, morals represent an individual's internal beliefs of right and wrong, a compass involving the heart and mind. Buddhist scriptures tell us of the Buddha's realizations upon his reaching enlightenment, realizations that became the ethical guidelines that he taught throughout his lifetime. And it is when we internalize these teachings, acting upon them not because they are rules set down by the Buddha, but because we understand how they can lessen our suffering and that of others, that morality develops. The Buddha gave us the seeds for our enlightenment, the cultivation of those seeds is our individual choice.

Morality is, therefore, something that we can nurture. Morality ensures that there will be law and order in a nation. When a nation loses its moral compass, people everywhere struggle with one another for their own benefit, profiting at the expense of others with no sense of shame. We become sick at heart. Thus, only by cultivating a sense of morality and by leading a moral life will society become harmonious, families find happiness, friends keep promises, and people help one another.

As mentioned in the previous chapter, for Buddhists, the six perfections provide the main criterion through which we can develop a moral life. And within this practice, the precepts, meditation, and wisdom offer a cure for the three poisons. If a person upholds the precepts, that person will not be selfish. Without selfishness, greed will not arise. By meditating, a person will learn not harm others. Without harm, anger will not arise. And if a person cultivates wisdom, ignorance can be eliminated. Once greed, anger, and ignorance are eliminated and a person practices charitable behavior, a benevolent and compassionate heart will manifest naturally.

History abounds with examples of people who lent their aid to others, and there are many modern-day heroes from whom we can learn. The *Los Angeles Times* once reported the story of a factory worker from Detroit who worked overtime and saved in order to donate thousands of dollars to various colleges and universities. Often we read about witnesses of accidents who risked their lives to help those who were hurt. While such people may not be Buddhists, their actions resonate with the Buddha's teachings. The common link among heroes is their ability to put the welfare of others ahead of their own. Their actions are not guided by personal gain but by altruism and peace of mind. These are all examples of putting the Dharma into practice, and each one of us can find ways to incorporate the Dharma into our everyday lives.

While it may be hard enough to be clear about what our goals should be, it is many times harder to develop the stamina to complete these goals. For example, you may find that ideas in this book are inspiring and resonate with you. You might wholeheartedly agree that these pages contain excellent suggestions about how to live a life of affinity. But these ideas and teachings are merely words on a page, unfruitful notions that exist in the mind and not in life. Spiritual development cannot progress if we only think about doing good, but do not put the teachings into practice and experience them firsthand. Furthermore, if we only experience the Buddha's teachings on an intellectual level with no opportunity for their wonders to manifest, we will wind up helping no one. Having mental clarity and good intentions are important steps, but following through is what will truly make a difference in our lives and in the lives of others.

How we treat others, therefore, is a matter of learning as well as an art. We should try to walk in another's shoes to truly understand their experience. Moreover, we should humbly learn from the strengths of others and be tolerant of their shortcomings. All in all, how we treat others hinges on meeting their needs with skill and consideration, as well as compassion and wisdom. The following are six points to consider:

1. *When people have a strong personality, win them over with gentleness.*

In dealing with others, if they are strong-minded and we are also firm and upright, the resulting clash of personalities will hurt both parties. Therefore, when the other person is riding high in their power, and taking a tough stand, we should win him or her over with gentleness. When we are yielding and tolerant, we will be able to gain harmony through patience.

2. *When people scheme, inspire them with sincerity.* Some people like to constantly conspire and plot. In dealing with such people, we should not imitate them, for when we become deceitful and crafty, we drain our energy and hurt everyone's feelings. Instead, we should treat them with sincerity.

3. *When people are angry, appease them with reason.* Some people react to situations impulsively, losing their tempers easily. So when they rely on anger, we should use reason to calm them. As the saying goes, "With reasoning, we can go anywhere. When we have reason on our side, we can win any debate and be able to stand firm."

4. *When people are deceitful, treat them with honesty.* Some people often speak dishonestly, acting without integrity. When dealing with people who are dishonest in both speech and action and we follow suit, we will find it hard to get along. Therefore, even when others try to deceive us, we should treat them with honesty. Only when we treat others with a true heart will friendships last.

5. *When people are malicious, repay them with kindness.* Those who regularly commit unrighteous acts will inevitably invite their own downfall. We should always have kind thoughts and practice benevolence in order

to increase our merits. Some people, however, often treat others with malice. If we, in turn, treat them the same, we are only stooping to their level. Therefore, even if others are malicious in their behavior, we should show them kindness. Treating people with a kind heart is the greatest benefit we can give to others.

6. *When people are volatile, steady them with firmness.* Some people are like weather vanes, constantly shifting with the wind and never settled. When others keep changing, we must remain firmly grounded. When we know how to face all changes without changing our stance, we will not lose our focus.

The path to Buddhahood is a long one. During the journey, we are bound to face obstacles, and it behooves us not to give up easily. If we do, it is just like sowing seeds without bothering to give them water and fertilizer. Without nurture and the test of time, the chance of a plant blooming and bearing fruit is minimal at best. Thus, if we are to complete the goal we set out to achieve, we should be willing to do the impossible task and walk the impossible walk. We need to keep in mind that understanding and practice are equally important, and by continually putting the Buddha's teachings into practice, one day we will discover that we and the Dharma are one. When we can generate the same compassion and the same aspiration for awakening as the bodhisattvas and cultivate the six perfections for our own benefit and that of others, the pure land of Humanistic Buddhism will appear before us.

I hope that I have succeeded in making the Dharma more relevant and accessible to you. Some believe that to be profound, teachings must be incomprehensible and cryptic. This is not the case at all. The Dharma is something that we can all understand and use as a guiding light to help us better evaluate the many and varied aspects of life. Buddhism is about life, and is inseparable from life.

Chapter Eight

On Society:
The Way of Oneself and Others

Human beings are social animals; we cannot live apart from community. As Buddhists, we are told to seek the Dharma among people, for the Dharma does not exist in some other world or faraway place; the Dharma is here among us, embodied in each and every being. Thus, Buddhists understand what many people of other religious traditions also know. The cornerstone of happy living rests on the development of good relationships and nurturing positive affinity with others. When we understand that human society is nothing other than a web of relationships, we will understand their true importance. Each link in the web, each person in a community affects the whole.

Relationships create a particular atmosphere within a community and determine whether the community—be it a neighborhood, a place of religious gathering, a family, or a different form of community—invites mutual benefit and harmony or leaves its members in a state of isolation and conflict. Once we see how the repercussions of even one relationship can impact an entire community, we will

65

learn to treasure each one and invest our most sincere and open efforts to create those that are healthy and beneficial. Wholesome actions generate the seeds of good relationships, while unwholesome actions breed problems with others. It is crucial to remember that we all play a key role in maintaining the health and well-being of this interlocking web.

Harmony and beauty within our lives and within our communities often fail due to our insistence on the duality of self and others. The ultimate solution for generating peace and accord in our relationships and in our world, therefore, lies in seeing that we all are one. Never-Disparaging Bodhisattva was always respectful to everyone he met, for he knew that we are all capable of becoming a Buddha one day. He did not maintain a dual, and therefore, erroneous perception that distinguished between people he deemed worthy of being treated with esteem and people he deemed unworthy. Through recognizing the interconnectedness of all beings, the perceived distance between us will shrink and an affirming environment will grow. If we all practice a modicum of this kind of regard for others, the world will be a much better place.

When we maintain the duality of self and others, we develop disproportionate levels of love and hatred, attraction and repulsion for other people, which throws our relationships out of balance. The capacity for affinity becomes dormant. We judge everyone around us, putting people into categories such as good and bad, acceptable and unacceptable. We want to spend time with those whom we love and accept, and we avoid socializing with those whom we dislike. Clinging to the notion of self and others causes these discriminating mindsets, and they disrupt the harmony and balance within a community.

If we replace this spirit of separateness with compassion, much of the friction in human relations will disappear. If we realize that we are all one, then there will be no impulse for jealousy and no room for conflict. There will be no inclination to like or dislike people. Everyone will be regarded with eyes of compassion. Through the eyes of oneness, we are never tempted to say that one group or one person is more important than the other. The *Diamond Sutra* teaches us that there is no boundary or chasm that separates self and others, and that we should seek to let go of this mental construct. Dissolving our dualistic world-view creates an environment in which natural affinity arises. When we practice viewing ourselves and others through a lens of oneness, we will no longer engage in meaningless mind-games that prevent us from forming positive connections with all beings.

Each of us, like a fine strand in a web, is part of the overall picture. Take a look at the five fingers of our hands. They are all different in length. Without these differences, we would not have the dexterity that we take for granted. A finger by itself cannot exert much force. However, if we combine the energy of the five fingers, our strength swells. Celebrating the differences in people while viewing everyone through the eyes of oneness nurtures powerful connections, creating a plane of existence where everyone is mutually supportive and respectful.

People from all walks of life, with different interests and inclinations, need to remember this sense of cooperation, including Buddhist practitioners from various schools. From one temple to another, from monastics to laity, we should embrace each other wholeheartedly and foster mutual respect. As long as we are supporting the purpose of the sangha, it does not matter what color our skin is or what school we follow. Under the umbrella of Buddhism, we all share a common teacher, the Buddha. And with equanimity, we should support each other in our common goal of spreading the Dharma. With open hearts and non-discriminating minds, we will seek the Dharma in all people, and like Never-Disparaging Bodhisattva, we will recognize the Buddha in every person.

Throughout history, we see that the differentiation of us versus them is the cause of many conflicts and wars. The Holocaust represents one of the ugliest examples. Likewise, in the Balkans, the atrocity of ethnic cleansing caused many large-scale tragedies. Instead of rejecting those who are different from us, we should learn to embrace them. The peace and harmony that develop from mutual respect and acceptance make the initial efforts all worthwhile. Instead of accentuating our differences, we should highlight our similarities. While we may look or act differently, we are fundamentally alike. After all, it is because we share similar causes and conditions that we were reborn in this world, at this time. All beings share an inherent connection, and we can either embrace or deny this, living in a manner that draws the connection out or leaves it dormant. We should treasure the similar conditions that bring us together as neighbors, friends and fellow inhabitants of this precious world.

The Buddhist sangha itself is a society. And though the Buddha stressed individual cultivation, he established the sangha to indicate that he considered relationships between the individual and society a serious matter. In Buddhism there is the expression: "Prosperity in the monastic community occurs when there are no conflicts." Only when people create harmony can they exist without conflict. The *Taking Refuge in the Triple Gem* ceremony states: "I take refuge in the Sangha, wishing that all sentient beings lead the public in harmony, without obstructions." The words "lead the public in harmony" simply mean to get along.

The sangha normally relies upon the six points of reverent harmonies to insure harmony:

1. Physical unity by living together
2. Verbal unity by not criticizing others
3. Mental unity through shared joy
4. Moral unity through upholding the same precepts
5. Doctrinal unity in views
6. Economic unity through sharing.

These six points are as applicable to lay society as they are to monastics. Much societal discord could be transformed into societal accord if all members of a community took these observances to heart. When we integrate the Buddha's teachings into daily life, the true beauty of relationships is revealed. We will directly experience the truth that affinity sings and discord grumbles.

In describing the Western Pure Land, the *Amitabha Sutra* mentions that, "All excellent people will congregate there." The reason for this is harmony, If a family is harmonious, that family will be happy; if a community is harmonious, that community will be peaceful. Subhuti was considered to be the best exponent of emptiness because of his realization of the *Samadhi of Non-contention*, in which there is no dispute or distinction between self and others. The *Vinaya* also emphasizes harmony. It contains seven rules for settling disputes among monastics, which serve as standards for harmony in the sangha.

Buddhism is a religion that focuses on human beings, and the Dharma provides solutions to nearly every human problem. For example, the *Numerical Discourses* provides methods for handling disputes between ourselves and others. It cautions people not to slander others or take notice of their faults but rather to examine ourselves and our own conduct to determine whether or not we are correct.

In addition, everyone hopes to build an exemplary reputation, but some people strive too hard. They do not hesitate to praise themselves while disparaging others. Through their excessive criticism, they not only establish harmful causes with others, but also to fall into telling lies, ironically giving themselves a negative reputation. In discussing what must be done to earn an exemplary reputation, the *Principles of the Six Perfections Sutra* teaches, "Do not disparage others and praise yourself. By not making distinctions between the self and others, one will earn a good name."

We should also keep in mind what the *Illuminating Light Sutra* says: "Do not repay hatred with hatred, eventually, it must stop." If hatred is repaid with hatred, there will be no end. Our only choice is to reciprocate with virtue, and in this way to cut off the roots of enmity. For example, the Buddha's cousin, Devadatta, always opposed the Buddha and on several occasions sought to harm him. One day Devadatta became ill, and all the physicians were powerless to help him. The Buddha himself came to see him and looked after him with great concern. The Buddha's exemplary behavior suggests, in the words of the *Principles of the Six Perfections Sutra*, "Not to recall others' negative deeds, but always to look at a person's positive side. The Buddha has wisdom that goes beyond distinctions. Therefore, he is the most enlightened of human beings."

Some people want to be better than others, because they are concerned with distinctions such as victory and defeat, which give rise to endless struggles. The *Dharmapada Sutra* states, "Victory breeds contempt, while defeat begets self-contempt. By ridding oneself of these distinctions, disputes will end and one will be at peace." So, if a person can respect another's greatness and, thereby, support and help another find fulfillment, that person can turn sadness into peace and happiness.

People also tend to strive to possess more than others, often ignoring others' needs. They seek a life of ease, single-mindedly pursuing their own happiness without considering the suffering of others. Even worse, many people prefer to blame others for their own mistakes, creating discord. If we can acknowledge our mistakes and negative behavior without blaming others and take responsibility for our own actions, then relations among people will be harmonious and without contention. As the *Collected Essential Teachings Sutra* says, "In the face of a violent person's unreasonable behavior and slander, the wise will only speak the truth and through patience, avoid trouble."

Communities should advocate watching out for and assisting one another, as well as strengthening relations among neighbors and caring for the aged. On this subject, the *Great Treasures Collection Sutra* remarks, "If a bodhisattva lives among people, he or she should teach the Dharma wherever he or she lives, be it village, city, prefecture, or county. He or she should lead the disbelievers to faith and the unfilial to filial piety. If people listen, he or she can persuade those who break the precepts to uphold them. Then the poor will have alms, the sick will have medicine, the defenseless will be protected, the homeless will have shelter, and the helpless will have assistance."

In any group, the most capable are those who can promote harmony. If people can smooth over their differences, then harmony can be achieved. Harmony comes with respect and forgiveness. As the *Flower Adornment Sutra* mentions, "When the Buddha spoke of the four means of embracing, all sentient beings in the ten directions were gladdened." They represent the best way to harmonize human relations. When we give charity, it makes no difference whether it is money and wealth or strength and words, it can gladden all and benefit our interactions with others. Praising, helping, and treating others equally are wonderful ways to handle our day-to-day affairs. The sutras teach us to form broad ties of good causes and conditions, which means we should not violate the rights of others nor let them down. Instead, we should endeavor to create beneficial conditions

for ourselves. Only by not violating the rights of others can we ensure harmonious relations.

Therefore, the relations between ourselves and others are two
sides of the same coin and are produced by mutually existing causes
and conditions. Each person is just one small part of the world. In
addition to myself, there is you, in addition to you, there is him or
her, and in addition to the three of us, there is everyone else. As we
move throughout our circles of interactions, there are three wise
considerations:

1. *Think of the greater good.*
   When we look at the world through the eyes of the
   community, our lives will be much more rewarding and
   joyful.
2. *Feel remorse for any harm that we cause.*
   When we're focused on our own faults, there is little
   room for delusion to manifest itself. When we do not
   dwell on the faults of others, there is little chance for
   conflicts to develop. In this way, we make peace, not
   war.
3. *Be generous and joyful.*
   If we understand that every cause has its effect, we may
   think differently about taking advantage of others, discover more reason for gratitude, and practice generosity.

Good relations between people in which there is help and fulfillment are a great blessing, while envy and rancor between people
lead to great unhappiness. The requisites for establishing positive
relationships with others include mutual respect, forgiveness, understanding, and assistance. And when we go beyond our external
differences, we will realize that they are but temporary shrouds that

cover our true nature. We will know that we are all the same and have the same Buddha nature. In this way, the perceived distance between people decreases and the chasm is crossed. When we remember that we are all of the same nature, then we will see that there is no reason that we cannot live together in harmony.

Part III

Staying on the Way

In life,

only at the moment of encountering
darkness,

can the preciousness of brightness be
displayed;

only when conducting oneself justly—
even while enduring slander,

can the fragrance of character be known.

— *Humble Table, Wise Fair*
Inspirtation

Chapter Nine

On Education and Entertainment: The Way of Mindful Living

Life is neither all work nor all cultivation. Like a plant that needs a balance of air, water, and sunlight to thrive; humans, too, need a variety of nutrients for their successful survival. Our lives are complex, and we cannot merely work or rest without some diversity and flexibility of experience. Therefore, in addition to three meals a day and attendance to responsibilities, the spiritual side of life must also be nourished through study and educational entertainment. With a little investigation, experimentation, and support from the sangha, our teachers, and our Dharma friends, we can discover our own balance of mind, body, and spirit.

In the Western Pure Land, mornings find those with baskets full of many wonderful flowers making offerings to the hundreds of thousands of millions of Buddhas of all directions. Throughout the day they rest amid seven rows of trees, seven tiers of railing, and the waters of the eight meritorious virtues, and proclaim the Buddha, the Dharma, and the Sangha, all of which provide joy for the body and mind.

The sangha, past and present, also gives us some excellent examples. When those who practice Chan sit in meditation, they must occasionally get up and walk around for the sake of the body and mind. Those who chant the Buddha's name will also want to circumambulate and venerate the Buddha. These simple, yet profound practices are sources of joy. And one day each week Buddhist monastics take a day off. At dinner they need not wear their ceremonial robes nor chant the Offering Dharani as they do for breakfast and lunch.

In the past, monastics were allowed to play chess as well as a game called "Picture of Becoming a Buddha." In this game, each of the six Chinese characters used to write the words "Namo Amitabha Buddha" had values for moving forward and backward, and moving into and out of the ten Dharma realms. Those who played the game not only increased their knowledge of Buddhism but also had a good time and enhanced their friendships with those practicing the Way. Monastics also practice the tea ceremony, calligraphy, carving, painting, and chanting, as well as debate the sutras and practice the art of transcribing the sutras. These are all educational ways to add a bit of spice to life.

Therefore, in addition to sleeping, eating, and working, appropriate forms of amusement are important for a change of pace. For most people, amusement involves running from one activity to the next, seeking pleasures that we hope will buy us a few moments of happiness. In contrast, Buddhism emphasizes experiences that exercise the body, and mind and encourage us to lean into the light of our Buddha nature. Chan masters, for example, have taught people to plant pine trees, pull weeds, and till the land, enabling their bodies to merge with nature in the fields and their senses to roam in the sea of the mind. Through simple activities we can find such a wealth of Dharma joy.

Among Buddhists, there are some who like to travel, sightsee, and make pilgrimages. Others prefer the outdoors, contemplating, meditating, and reflecting in solitude. For example, the *Contemplation of the Buddha of Infinite Life Sutra* lists the sixteen contemplations that include observing sunrise, sunset, mountains, rivers, trees, scenery, and Buddhas. Through these experiences, we can find a blending of contemplation into practice, practice into joy, and joy into peace, offering us endless opportunities for variety and expression in our lives.

From ancient times, Buddhism has placed an equal emphasis on five types of education: practicing together in the temples for morality, listening to the sutras for wisdom, doing chores for physical health, following the six points of reverent harmony of the sangha for group education, and practicing carving, painting, singing and chanting for aesthetic education. Today, Buddhism offers devotees many ways of practicing while having fun, clustered into the following six, general categories:

1. *Athletics*: Walking meditation, making pilgrimages to various temples, traveling, and practicing martial arts.
2. *Music*: Choir, playing musical instruments, traditional music, and storytelling.
3. *Arts*: Calligraphy, sutra transcription, painting, carving, sculpture, and chess.
4. *Flowers and tea*: Flower arrangement and the tea ceremony.
5. *Labor*: Working in nature, farming, working meditation, vegetable gardening, ascetic practice, and cooking.
6. *Practicing and upholding the Way*: Looking for teachers, discussing the Way, reciting the Buddha's name, and meditating, all leading to Chan joy and Dharma happiness.

Therefore, besides clothing, food, being comfortable, and enjoying the material side of life, we can enhance life through art, service, and rest. As you might have already surmised, the key lies not in any ancient, esoteric teaching but in the concept of Dharmakaya itself. Dharmakaya refers to the Buddha and to the Way which surrounds and supports us, and to the potential of our own Buddha nature. From this perspective, everything is Dharma and and Dharma permeates everything.

Any sort of amusement is appropriate as long as we do not give in to activities that cause harm. For example, we can enjoy early morning exercise, music before bed, or taking walks and strolls in our free time. Two or three good friends can get together to travel, chat, drink tea, talk about the Way, transcribe sutras, cook, or play music. Even dance and dinner parties among friends are acceptable.

From the beginning, Buddhism has placed an emphasis on peaceful cultivation in temples and monasteries. This sometimes strikes people as a cold and lonely practice, devoid of any feeling of human warmth. Many non-Buddhists think that Buddhism teaches emptiness, suffering, and the impermanence of all things to the detriment of joy in life. For this reason, they think that the true study of Buddhism involves cutting ourselves off from the real world. Actually, Buddhism is actively integrated into all areas of life. It is a religion of vigor and stresses interaction with others. Therefore, everything from walking, sitting, and sleeping to dressing, eating, caring for family, and working are all forms of the Dharma and open to the joy of the present moment.

Through the spiritual lens of Humanistic Buddhism, we should delve deeply into the scriptures in search of knowledge, while remembering that daily activities are also imbued with the Dharma. All we need to do is apply ourselves a little more in daily life to understanding, practicing, and experiencing this truth. Our lives will, then, be one with Dharma happiness rather than grounded in the ordinary happiness of the world.

What I have been moving toward in this chapter is a discussion of time. Can we find time, save time, or buy time to enhance our lives? In reality, despite a common, momentary perspective that time is dragging on, the truth is, time waits for no one, and time is precious. We can establish a foolish relationship with time or a wise one, a wasteful relationship or one in which productivity increases a thousandfold, a relationship that promotes a bond with others or one that hinders it, a relationship that is based only on brevity or one that embraces eternity. These choices are all in our hands.

One of the sutras teaches, "We live from breath to breath." This saying reminds us of the brevity and impermanence of life. Even though the mythical Peng Zu, for example, might have lived for eight hundred years, and the lifespan of heavenly beings extends to tens of thousands of years, such lifespans when viewed in the context of eternity are as fleeting as the morning dew. By living mindfully, it is possible to establish a relationship with time in which we are only living in utmost harmony and maximizing its use for the benefit of all beings. We can explore how to build this kind of relationship with time in the following three points.

1. Use Every Bit of Time

Some of us live to seventy, while others may live to be a hundred. Regardless, our limited time in this world is diminished by all kinds of activities that we must do to stay alive. Because of these activities, a twenty-four hour day is often chopped up into bits and pieces. We eat, sleep, carry out our jobs, take care of our families, and work around the house. Before we know it, another day is over.

If we deduct from our limited years the time we spend eating, sleeping, traveling from place to place, waiting in lines, cleaning ourselves, and going to the bathroom, how much time is left? On top of this, if we deduct our infancy and the time we will spend debilitated by old age, there is really not that much time left to apply ourselves to the betterment of humankind. The prime years of our lives are truly brief.

In this day and age of cell phones and iPads, time often becomes more intense, and life moves at an incredible pace. We try to multitask, completing several chores at once in an attempt to save time. And with the advent of increasingly portable technology, the nine-to-five workday is a thing of the past. Life becomes so packed with deadlines and schedules that every second counts. We can easily lose sight of our purpose and forget why we busied ourselves in the first place.

Some people say it is a blessing to be busy and feel needed, but are we preoccupied for the right reasons? For example, some people focus only on themselves and cannot give others the time of day. Others give their jobs their all and neglect their family. In today's fast-paced society, if we don't know how to make use of every bit of time, we will find ourselves always struggling for more. Employing this perspective, we can eliminate much struggle and skillfully adapt more successfully to a hectic lifestyle.

But given our fragmented days and years, and knowing how important it is for us to make wise choices about each moment, how do we do so? I often encourage people to become more mindful. In the case of young students, I advise them to make use of the fifteen minutes they have here and there to read a book, write in a journal, or review a chapter. Why waste time chatting or watching television? We can also recite Amitabha Buddha's name while cleaning, cooking, waiting for the bus or commuting to the workplace. These are excellent practices to begin at a young age, for society moves at a rapid pace.

While there is hardly enough time to do everything when we are young, the opposite is true as we move into later life. Building upon a lifetime of practice, we can still fill our time with the Dharma. Chanting the Buddha's name when physical activity is difficult or unfeasible is an excellent way for a senior citizen to spend time. I also suggest that we develop the habit of reading when we are young. Then, when we are less mobile we can always sit back with a good book. We can keep the mind young by keeping it busy and engaged. When our eyes are tired, we can recite the Buddha's name. When we are mindful of the Buddha, the Buddha will always be in our heart.

There is a Buddhist saying that we can use as a guide: "Say one less sentence, recite one more time the name of Amitabha Buddha." The utility of this simple phrase covers a multitude of circumstances. For example, when we carelessly chat with our friends, we may unthinkingly say something that offends them. So when we have a moment of free time, we could, instead, make use of it to recite the name of Amitabha Buddha or to contemplate the splendid appearance of the Buddha. Conversely, when we are busy, we can recite Amitabha's name to calm our minds. Amitabha is the Buddha of infinite light and infinite life and a good anchor in the ups and downs of life. Chanting his name is an effortless way to practice, a truly win-win situation. As we become more mindful of the Buddha, we will be at peace with whatever we are doing.

When we began to build Fo Guang Shan Temple in Taiwan many years ago, skeptics asked me, "Are you an architect? What do you know about construction? Are you a trained educator? What do you know about running schools?" I told them that my biggest secret was that I knew how to use my time. Even though I am not an architect or a trained educator, I have traveled to many places and have seen many houses and temples. Therefore, when involved with construction projects, I often put myself in the shoes of the building contractor and imagined what I would do. This perspective served me well. At the outset of the temple's initial construction phase, I already had a plan, and through using my time wisely, everything just fell into place. I was in tune with my capacity, the capacity that everyone has to accomplish great things in the face of fleeting time.

Unfortunately, when I look around, I see many people unconsciously wasting their time. There is an art to managing time, and balancing the demands of our material and spiritual needs. We must look out for ourselves, while considering the well-being of others. And we must work for the present as well as the future. If we can create a balance between these areas, then we will manage our time well, and we will not have squandered a precious moment.

2. Seize the Present Moment

The passing of time is inevitable and merciless. If we are not watchful, time slips by without a trace, like a thin veil of fog or columns of clouds in the sky. If we wait for things to happen, we often end up sitting idly by. We should work to better ourselves and others, for we do not want to look back when we are old and wish that our lives had been different.

We should seize the present moment and make things happen. As long as we have the ability to do good, we should act whenever an opportunity presents itself. In fact, we can be proactive with our time and actually create such opportunities. We do not want to look back and think about what could have been if only we had not procrastinated. If we are wise, we will not romanticize the past or fantasize about the future. We will simply live in the present, making the best use of our time.

The site we chose for the Fo Guang Shan Temple in Taiwan was a remote and barren piece of land. Some questioned why we were wasting our time. But if we had not started when we did, or if we had decided to wait for a better location, the temple might not be here today. If we had chosen a different relationship with time—one of scarcity instead of abundance—then we would not have accomplished our goal. We would not have maintained the confidence that there was enough time to complete such a massive project. But if we develop our affinity with time, and if we use time to create rather than to wait, we can turn dreams into reality. When we dedicate ourselves to serving others, our time is well spent.

3. *Realize Eternity through the Brevity of Life*

If we only focus on the brevity of our life, we will begin to think that life is dull and lacks possibilities. We will constantly be hindered by perceived boundaries and miss opportunities to help others and do good in the world. Conversely, if we realize that the true span of our life is everlasting, then life becomes a lot more interesting and is suddenly rich with possibilities. Some of you may think that since we will all die one day, it is impossible that life is everlasting. Let me explain. We tend to think that our time begins when we are born and ends when we die. Because of this tunnel vision and our attachment to the world of phenomena, we do not realize that our being is much larger than physical manifestation. When we begin to view existence within the context of the cycle of rebirth, we realize that we have a long history and an unbounded future.

Our physical body is like a house. When the house is beyond repair, we move on to a new one. When our bodies grow old and die, we will move into a new body. Of course, the kind of body we take up will depend upon our cumulative good and bad karma. Therefore, if we can break out of our insular mindset, we will understand that death is, in fact, the beginning of another life. The Buddha teaches us that life is without beginning and without end. Life is the culmination of causes and conditions, and as such it is continually changing. Like the water in a fast-running river, it is never the same water. As soon as some water flows away, more comes to take its place.

Impermanence is an inherent characteristic of the natural world. Look around. We all experience birth, aging, and death. Likewise, the inanimate world is marked with becoming, existing, deteriorating, and ceasing. The sutras say, "Mount Sumeru may be huge and tall, yet it will disappear one day. Despite the great depths of the sea, it will become dry when its time is up. Though the sun and moon shine brightly, they will cease to exist before long. The great earth may be strong and holds all there is, but when the fire of karma burns at the end of the kalpa, it, too, cannot escape impermanence." When we see this truth, we will no longer fear death and rebirth. While our form or our "house" may be different for each rebirth, our Buddha nature remains the same. Unfortunately, many of us do not know our Buddha nature, our true insight. As we course through the cycles of death and rebirth, we become attached to the impermanence of self-image and lose touch with this intrinsic part of our being.

If we could look into the past and future, we would realize that many of the myriad relationships in this world are both pitiful and laughable because they are not viewed in the context of the eternal continuity of time and life or the endless cycle of rebirth. The *Inspiration for the Bodhicitta Pledge* speaks of two such examples: "Whipping the mule until it bleeds, who knows of my mother's sorrow?" and "Taking the animal to be slaughtered, how do I know of your father's pain?" There is a story behind these two lines.

Once there was family who had a mule. For many years, the family used the mule to pull produce to the market. When the mule grew old, it was no longer strong enough to pull the cartloads of produce. The mule's owner thought that he could get some more use out of it if only he could show the mule who was master. Every day he whipped the mule so that it would work harder.

One night, he dreamed that the mule appeared before him in human form pleading, "In your previous life, I was your mother. I was not a good mother and neglected you. As a result, I was reborn as a mule to repay my debt. For the last twenty years, I have helped you transport produce to the market. Now that I am old and weak, I can no longer work as before. Please have pity on me and spare me your whipping."

When the man awoke, he was ashamed that he had been so cruel, and took the mule to a nearby temple where it could live out its days in peace. That day he gained a greater understanding of the cycle of rebirth and the continuity of life and became more skilled at offering compassion to his fellow beings.

This story enables us to take the rebirth analogy of moving into a new house a step further. If we have been putting money away while living in our current house, then we can afford to move to a nicer, bigger house when the current one starts to fall apart. If we have not put money away, when it is time to leave we will have no choice but to move to a smaller house. Thus, while our lifespan is limited, we should use our time wisely to act compassionately and do good. By steadfastly practicing during our brief existence, we will undergo a favorable rebirth. This insight is why Buddhists do not fear death, and why we do not look at death as the final chapter of life.

Let me tell you another story. Once, there was an elderly gentleman who wanted to plant a peach tree. As he was laboring to plant the small tree, a young man passed by. Striking up a conversation with the elderly gentleman he asked, "Sir, are you sure you want to spend so much energy planting this tree? You may not live to see it grow, let alone enjoy it's fruit. Is this not a waste?"

The old man stood up and wiped off his sweat. He looked at the young man and with a dry, crackling voice replied, "You are too young to understand the meaning of life. I am not planting this tree for myself. Though I may not live to see it bear fruit, my sons will get to enjoy its shade, and my grandchildren will enjoy its fruit. How can you say this is a waste?"

The young man was moved by the profound insight of the elderly gentleman. The older man knew that later generations would enjoy the fruits of the labor of earlier generations, and he acted accordingly. We, too, should look at the larger life of the universe. While a person's life may only span a limited number of years, its value is everlasting.

The continuity of life from one lifetime to the next is not unlike the process of fire spreading from one log to another. While the fire of the second log is not the same as the first, it represents a continuation of the fire from the first log. In a similar way, from one rebirth to the next we can see the continuity of life. Affinity also transcends a single lifespan. Its energy flows through life's continuity. By building affinity in this lifetime, we will pass it along our next life and to future generations.

Given that we all play linking roles in the continuum of life, how are we to contribute to this larger life? Some people contribute through politics, others through their writing, still others through their own example. While these are all worthwhile contributions, Buddhism teaches us a more complete and supreme way. Buddhism teaches that when we discover our own Dharmakaya and our own balance, we will have found eternity. Dharmakaya is everywhere and everlasting.

Our great teacher, Sakyamuni Buddha, is the primary example of one who found eternity in the Dharmakaya. Though the Blessed One entered final nirvana over 2,500 years ago, the Dharmakaya of the Buddha is still here with us. The way we spend each moment is significant, and our practice has always been significant, spanning from the past into the future. This is the meaning of eternity in life and the ultimate example of affinity with each other and with time.

Chapter Ten

On Long Life, Wealth, and Happiness:
The Way of Ownership

Long life and happiness are sought by all. Everyone hopes to be financially comfortable, to be treated respectfully, to live long, and to be happy. However, more often than not, attaining both long life and happiness proves to be difficult. A person might be richer than the nation, yet die young, while another might live to be as old as Methuselah but be poor and downtrodden all of his or her life.

Within the concepts of happiness and longevity, finances often figure prominently. In today's complex societies, we all need some amount of capital to survive. But are we content with our material possessions, or do we always crave more? Are we grateful for what we have or do we take it all for granted? Are we able to distinguish between our needs and our wants? Are we using our wealth for the benefit of others, or for our own personal desires? These are important questions to consider as we examine our relationship to the material world and learn how to build a positive affinity with this aspect of our lives.

The clothing we wear, the food we eat, the accommodations we live in, the transportation we rely on, the finances we deal with, and so forth are all part of our existence. Our relationships with these things can be positive or negative, harmonious or discordant, harmful or beneficial, ignorant or mindful. When we are living with positive affinity, one dollar is a blessing; when we lack such affinity, even a million dollars is not enough. A healthy affinity with the material aspect of life will help us maintain a balance and a helpful attitude about possessions and money.

In regard to how we should manage our material wants and needs, Buddhism does not suggest that we unduly deprive ourselves. While a life of extreme self-mortification is spiritless and dull, Buddhism also stresses that we should not be self-indulgent in our material needs and wants. From one desire to another, we can become enslaved to the material world at the expense our our spiritual development. Thus, Buddhism does not endorse either a life of self-mortification or one of self-indulgence, a stance well documented in the sutras.

For example, while the *Amitabha Sutra* speaks of inconceivable comfort in the Western Pure Land, the environment is only a means for furthering the practice of the Dharma and attaining Buddhahood. It is by no means an invitation to complacency and gluttony. When the *Diamond Sutra* says, "Let intentions arise without any clinging," it tells us that we need not give up everything. Instead, it stresses the practice of the Middle Way.

But does choice in the present moment alone determine our current life's circumstances? While most of us wish for a comfortable life, not all of us will come into riches. Due to the law of cause and effect, only those who have planted the karmic seeds of wealth are blessed with wealth. Wealth is not something that is bestowed by the gods, but the fruit of past generosity. While alms-giving is the seed of wealth, hard work is the condition that nurtures the seed to fruition. Therefore, our past impacts our present and that we cannot change. But we can definitely influence the future by our present actions. When we give our time, our life, or our compassion, we are also giving alms. We all possess the ability and means to plant the karmic seeds of wealth.

Unfortunately, for some of us the temptation of money and the ways in which we use it may lead us to compromise our integrity and damage our precocious relationships. We frequently read about family feuds that developed due to conflict over the distribution of an inheritance. If ethics are abandoned as we manage and relate to our finances, we are laying the foundation for future suffering and moral bankruptcy, even if our actual bank accounts are overflowing. So how do we manage our finances prudently to ensure that our ethics remain intact?

I would like to offer a Buddhist perspective on the acquiring, using, and measuring of wealth. The resulting positive affinity could engender spiritual development as well as healthy relationships with others. At the same time, we will learn how to build a foundation for good fortune. Again, we turn to the sutras. In the words of the *Great Treasures Collection Sutra,* "Lay bodhisattvas may accumulate wealth, but it must be done so in accordance with the Dharma." What this means is that as we make a living, we must acquire that which is right by working and living in accordance with the Noble Eightfold Path. Here, the Buddha teaches us about right livelihood and the importance of the five precepts. He instructs that we should earn our living with integrity and ethics, avoiding businesses that involve gambling or the buying and selling of intoxicants, living beings, or arms. We need to give careful consideration to our means of acquiring wealth.

Wealth by itself has no ethical value. It is the immoral pursuit and acquisition of wealth, along with its ill use that causes difficulties.

Money, if used properly, can be applied to the betterment of society, a resource for spreading the Dharma. For example, if we want to encourage new generations to engage in this work, we need to provide a good education for the young by setting up schools. This takes money. We need to hire teachers, which also takes money. Thus, whether money, once acquired, becomes a poison or a tool depends upon how it is used.

On an individual level, our money can be invested in providing security for our parents, providing a comfortable living for our spouses and children, offering our children quality education, expanding our earning potential, saving for retirement, and making charitable donations. While this is not an exhaustive list, these ideas can serve as guidelines for wise and considerate spending. The appropriate way to apportion wealth in these categories depends on each person's unique circumstances.

In order to truly understand the importance of wealth, we also need insight into its measurement. What is the nature of wealth? How do we know when we have reached success? Some people measure affluence by their material possessions or the size of their bank accounts. Actually, the amount of money that we have does not determine happiness. Wealth solves many problems, but also creates new ones. True, the rich may never worry about their next meal, but they can be burdened by complex social and legal issues. Happiness depends more on our personal integrity and how we feel about ourselves, as well as the quality of our relationships.

Even the Buddha participated in the material world and had basic needs to be met. Yet, he shows us by example how to relate to our wealth. The Buddha was just as happy with a simple robe as with a royal garment. He enjoyed the food that he collected from his alms rounds as much as the food that was offered to him as a guest of honor. He felt at content sleeping under a tree or in a palace. The

Buddha was always at ease with his circumstances. The distinctions of rich and poor had no bearing on his inner peace. Therefore, if we measure wealth only by material possessions, we will not feel content and satisfied. Desire is a bottomless pit, often playing out in a game of wants rather than absolute needs. Regardless of how much we own, if we do not have inner peace, we will always desire more.

We should also remember that in the physical world, everything is subject to impermanence. Wealth and poverty are no exceptions. Wealth can disappear, and people can go from rags to riches. While we say, "This is mine," or "I possess this," the relationship we have with our wealth is, actually, much more tenuous. Even death teaches us this lesson. We come into this world empty-handed, and we will leave the same way. The sutras say, "We cannot take anything with us; only karma shadows us everywhere." While this sounds obvious, many of us do not take it to heart. Therefore, a lack of insight into the nature and measurement of wealth can also affect our wellbeing, even at life's closing.

How, then, can we cultivate the causes of long life and happiness? According to Buddhist beliefs, neither the heavens nor any authority on earth bestows this upon us. Instead, our own karma determines happiness and longevity. We reap what we sow, if you will. But Buddhism's five precepts inspire the inner force of self-regulation, helping us to be mindful of our current actions, and to create positive change in our lives. Their fundamental spirit is to not harm others. When we do not harm others, we will have freedom. Therefore, fully upholding the five precepts leads to happiness and long life.

The *Great Teacher King Sutra* states, "Happiness and long life are desired; they are attained when karma ripens. We can cultivate our blessedness in all fields of merit, by respecting the Triple Gem, parents, and teachers; teaching disciples; and helping the ill, the physically handicapped, and victims of disaster." Therefore, the karma of happiness and long life are also inextricably linked to the cultivation and kindness of the heart. If we can form relationships with others and cultivate the necessary causes, happiness and longevity will follow naturally. Knowingly doing harm, might gain us momentary success, but disaster will quickly follow. For example, a person might obtain temporary happiness by stealing someone's wealth, but after the crime is revealed, he or she will be punished. Such behavior is more akin to licking honey from a knife. So while good causes remain dormant, one must persevere in benevolence and compassion, and disaster will eventually turn to blessings.

Though the causes and effects that lead to happiness and long life are discussed in the sutras, some people believe that they should pray to the gods, the bodhisattvas, and the Buddha instead. Their faith rests on a longing for having and taking more than they need. The *Dharmapada Sutra* tells us, "Seeking happiness by worshiping the gods, one waits for the rewards. Getting no results, one would be better off respecting the sage." Therefore, simply having the desire for happiness and long life, does not guarantee their attainment. Without cultivation of the appropriate causes and conditions, such desires will not manifest. There is a saying that "Being born in heaven, one must have achieved the necessary causes and conditions, but one will not necessarily become an immortal by seeking to be one." This means that if we merely place the burden for our happiness and long life on the Buddha, we are not living in accordance with the law of karma. This would be like placing a heavy stone in the water and expecting it to float. Everything is dependent upon whether we ourselves diligently sow the necessary karmic seeds.

Traditional Chinese culture notes five blessings that descend upon a house: happiness, status, wealth, long life, and joy. These constitute blessings for most people, but if we possess all five types of blessings, will life be perfect and without regrets? And is blessings in life limited to these five types? Does their achievement guarantee a life free of worry and trials?

Actually, as everything has its cause and effect, and long life and happiness contain their own shortcomings. For example, people often comment enviously to others, "You have a happy lot in life." Perhaps. But happiness and worry exist side by side in all areas of life. When our children are young, for instance, we worry about their health and growth. When they're grown, we worry about their success or failure. Even after they become adults with careers and relationships, we worry about their satisfaction at home and whether their careers are progressing smoothly. And the more children, the more happiness and worries we feel. Likewise, the more wealth we acquire, the more worries we seem to encounter. With money, one can enjoy security, well-being, and all manner of pleasures. But at times money can also bring unexpected troubles. Happiness and worry are as closely linked as a body to its own shadow.

Longevity and the nature of old age are inseparable as well. In Chinese culture, we often say: "May you live to be a hundred," and even, "May you live to be one hundred and twenty." But if a person actually lived that long, his or her children, eighty-year old grandchildren, and sixty-year-old great-grandchildren may have all already passed away. Who would take care of us? How would we live?

Therefore, Buddhism does not necessarily consider old age to be free of suffering or a goal that we ought to pursue. At the same time, Buddhism does not deny the pursuit of long life and happiness. Rather, Buddhism advocates, "In pursuing happiness, pursue the happiness of wisdom. Only then will there be merit. In pursuing long life, pursue a long life with more compassion." Happiness without wisdom is as difficult as driving a car that is missing a wheel, or flying a plane with one wing. Only the happiness of wisdom will allow us to give that same happiness to all sentient beings. By the same token, to live a long life without doing good has no lasting significance. For this reason, we should seek the happiness of wisdom and compassion in old age.

When one considers long life, it is important to keep in mind that there is the present life, the next life, and countless future lives. It is the same as the withering and fading of fruit and flowers. Life will continue as long as the seeds are sown. Although the human body is a result of karma and subject to conditions and has a beginning and an end, the value of life holds no such limits and is eternal. Thus, in pursuing long life, we should pursue infinite life, a life which transcends time and space. We can begin to imagine this perspective by noting some other forms of long life.

1. *The lifespan of a family enterprise.* This might include establishing a business, factories or companies that extend benefits to all of society. Such enterprises might be managed for several decades or even a century.

2. *The lifespan of a culture.* The preciousness of human life is found in the transmission of the words and deeds of our ancestors, and in all manner of historical experience.

3. *The lifespan of teachings.* Teachings from the past represent the inherited wisdom of humankind and a cultural treasure house. Culture is thus renewed like adding fuel to a low-burning fire, and the lifespan of teachings transcends time and space.

4. *The lifespan of faith.* Cultures emphasize the idea of handing things down from one generation to the next. Faith can also be transmitted throughout generations, as one lamp lighting the next.

5. *The lifespan of morality.* Sages throughout history have dedicated and sacrificed themselves for benevolence and justice. The morality handed down by the ancients can lend us guidance.

6. *The lifespan of wisdom.* A life of wisdom is a life of liberation and purity. Such a life includes joy, selflessness, compassion, and the limitless merit of wisdom.

7. *The lifespan of merit.* Erecting halls and Buddhist images; printing books on Buddhism, planting trees, offering food; and other meritorious deeds are acts to be cherished and blessings for which our descendants can be proud. The heritage left by the monastic community has been to change and influence by practicing and upholding the Way. In addition to raising their lives to a higher spiritual level, they also strengthen the faith of future generations of believers. This pure, non-material merit is eternal.

8. *The lifespan of coexistence.* The ideals of caring for others and developing personal relations are deeply rooted in Buddhism. Today, this also includes loving and caring for the earth. These insights will help future generations enjoy peace, happiness, and a collective life of ease.

We must remain ever mindful of our actions. If we live to be one hundred and twenty and are extremely wealthy, what have we really acquired? How much leisure time did we enjoy? Although we have many enterprises, can we rely upon them? Are our family members close to us? The passage of time shows all too often that our statuses, possessions, and acquisitions do not guarantee joy and ease. The ways in which we choose to live our lives and work toward our goals is crucial.

The *Dharmapada Sutra* remarks, "Better to live one day pursuing the Dharma than one hundred years without the supreme truth."

Though we might live to be the age of Methuselah, old age, sickness, death, and rebirth are inevitable; and happiness is as rare as being a king or winning the lottery. Therefore, when we seek happiness, we must strive for eternal happiness, life after life, and not the momentary happiness of this life. The *Diamond Sutra* teaches that the "happiness of this life is limited, comes to an end, and has causes and outflows. Eternal happiness is limitless and has no end or outflows, nor can it be stolen, burned or lost."

Therefore, daily life needs order. We should strive to maintain a calm and happy state of mind and not be easily angered. We must be diligent in obtaining new knowledge and skills, establishing enterprises, serving society, and improving our lives by living the Buddha's teachings. By enriching our life, there will be no room for afflictions, and we can enjoy a happy life at peace.

Wealth gives us a material opportunity to practice the positive aspects of Buddhist morality in this world. Through the thoughtful acquisition and generous use of wealth we can learn non-attachment, compassion, generosity, and clear thinking. In the end, the greatest wealth of all is the knowledge of our own Buddha nature. One glimpse of the abundant spiritual wealth that lies within you is worth more than all of the material wealth in the universe.

Today's world is complicated; our lives are complicated. Yet, we all have such potential! In addition to managing time and using it to benefit society and extend our own lifespan, we should be diligent in creating lasting, beautiful language; good morals; and an incorruptible culture. We should strive to develop illustrious enterprises, firm faith, pure wisdom, eternal virtue, and a life of community. These are the efforts that will carry us across the threshold of the path toward true happiness and long life.

Chapter Eleven

On Government and International Affairs: The Way of Participation and Tolerance

We live in incredible times. Owing to ever-increasing, techno-logical advances, global communications have become more widespread and sophisticated. Varied forms of satellite communication now link people across the world, making the twenty-first century the age of the global village. Now, it is the diversity of the global population that drives progress as peoples of different nations, cultures, and languages possess the means to join their efforts as never before.

Throughout the nations, cities, and towns of the world there are many communities. Within each community, we find households, families, personalities, ages, genders, languages, customs, and religious beliefs subsisting side by side. These smaller, more intricate patterns of relationship begin with a love of family, then broaden to include neighbors, village, society, nation, humankind, and all sentient beings. The closer the relationship is, the deeper the love and commitment. The more distant the relationship, the weaker the bond. Thus, the ideal of unconditional loving-kindness and great compassion to all, advocated by Buddhism, is actually difficult for most people to practice.

The causes and conditions of love and compassion radiate complexity, especially when it comes to our relatives, the distinctions between love and hate, and the distinctions we imagine between ourselves and others. As a result, haggling, disputes, and fighting often arise within our most significant relationships. Regarding international relations, Humanistic Buddhism seeks to eliminate the drawing of distinctions, advocating an awareness of oneness and the coexistence of mutual tolerance, respect, equality, cooperation, and sharing.

The *Amitabha Sutra* speaks of the Western Pure Land stating that, "Each living being of that land, with baskets full of many wonderful flowers, makes offerings to the hundreds of thousands of millions of Buddhas of all directions." This forming of ties and mutual praise represent a fully international view found in many Buddhist scriptures. For example, the *Ascent of Maitreya Sutra* and the *Descent of Maitreya Sutra*, tell us that the Maitreya Buddha not only interacts with the people of our world, but also with those in the three realms, the twenty-eight heavens, and the eighteen hells, where he liberates countless beings. In addition, Never-Disparaging Bodhisattva treats all sentient beings without distinction, and Avalokitesvara Bodhisattva travels through all lands fulfilling his vows of liberation.

When eating, Buddhists make offerings to all sentient beings. For the smallest things, we thank all beings in the ten directions, recognizing our oneness. Buddhism advocates equality, and is particularly concerned about small, powerless groups and underdeveloped nations. The Buddhist scriptures bring this point home to our hearts by relating that the Buddha treated all sentient beings as if they were Rahula, his beloved son. Thus, Buddhism stresses equality and protecting the right to life for all sentient beings.

People say that since ancient times, those who have traveled the world have included soldiers, merchants, explorers, and Buddhist monastics seeking teachers and the Way. One history of the relations between China and India relates the story of the thousands of Buddhist monastics and lay followers who walked the Silk Road. Another history of the relations between China and Japan, tells of the great numbers of people who crossed the sea between the two countries. And one Mahayana scripture states, "To embrace three thousand worlds in one thought, the mind contains the great universe." Thus, the Buddhist world-view eliminates distinctions of time and space.

In the thirty years since tourism was first widely encouraged in Taiwan, Buddhists have organized tours to all parts of the world. With contact across the Taiwan Strait, Taiwanese Buddhists have flocked to China to make pilgrimages to famous mountain temples. I have led a number of groups to India, Nepal, and the United States and once designed a ten-stage plan for visiting different part of the world. In addition, Fo Guang Shan often organizes international academic conferences and trips, such as a trip to the Vatican to meet with the Pope and trips to mosques, all with the hopes of sowing peace throughout the world.

I once said that because Taiwan was able to develop its science and technology, it enjoys prosperity, but only in a material sense. Spiritual poverty, chaos, and sickness have also spread. Buddhists emphasize internal purity, thereby recognizing that the roots of such afflictions in the world stem from ignorance and clinging to the notion of a self. The human desires for power and fame are also rooted there, as is greed that leads to conflict and perpetual struggle. Buddhism teaches us that in order to heal the chaos in the world we must start by purifying the mind. World peace is possible only by realizing peace within, and by practicing the Buddhist teachings of non-self, compassion and respect for all.

The United Nations is an untiring voice for peace, and peace is the dream of every person. Buddhism sees the ideal of one family under heaven as establishing a pure land on earth. In addition to protecting human rights, Buddhism goes one step further by considering that all sentient beings have the right to life. Buddhism respects this right because all sentient beings possess Buddha nature, and all are future Buddhas. This kind of advocacy transcends national boundaries to view our world as one beyond all divisions, one in which we are equal.

The *Subcommentary on the Flower Adornment Sutra* teaches, "The mind, the Buddha, and all sentient beings are the same." Mutual respect, forgiveness, equality, non-self, and compassion between sentient beings are the ideals needed by all peoples and nations. Because we all reside on this earth, we should have the same hope of living together and promoting the idea of equality between the Buddha and sentient beings, the sage and the ordinary person, ourselves and others, thereby eliminating the divisions between peoples and nations.

We could, therefore, benefit from adopting the international perspective of extending our awareness throughout the ten directions and the three time periods, using the concept of the world as a single family as a reference point. This will enable us to embrace the dharma realms and become citizens of the world, protecting the environment and caring for all resources. By treating others as we would like to be treated, we can enlighten ourselves as well as others, improve life, foster faith, form good affinities with all sentient beings, act compassionately, and bring light to the world. Only in this way can we promote world peace together.

All rhetoric aside, can the ideas of non-self, loving-kindness, and compassion really engender actions leading to world peace? Let us delve a little deeper into our hearts and minds for further illumination. Non-self does not mean that the concept of "I" is nonexistent or that there is no self. Rather, non-self means being able to break down and eliminate the attachments to my ideas, my opinions, my beliefs, and what I want to do. Since this world belongs to no single person but is held in common by all, we must respect and tolerate the ideas, opinions, and aspirations of others. Loving-kindness and compassion mean treating others well, and it is easier to do so when we work to develop some understanding of another's point of view. Therefore, these concepts are far from trivial, and their expansion and development can, indeed, lead to world peace.

To further explain, as all life is interconnected, humanity can only attain peace through solidarity and friendship. In this context, solidarity means extending the hand of friendship, rather than passively waiting for others to join us. Peace means that we are at peace with others, not that we expect others to bring peace to us. Anything that requires others to do something first will be harder to achieve. Peace begins when each of us takes the initiative to develop goodwill. Positive effects will only arise from positive causes. This is the law of karma. Every country should attempt to be trustworthy, virtuous, and act with loving-kindness, compassion, joy, and equanimity. Each state should strive to be tolerant of what differs from themselves, refrain from invading and subjugating others, and communicate with others in the spirit of non-self.

No one should lose faith in peace. Did the Berlin Wall, the very epitome of stony hostility, not come down? War and peace are human constructions. If our hearts remain full of hatred, and we spend our time thinking about how to subdue others, world peace will be impossible. What matters most is our commitment to the principle of equality for all living beings. Only when we hold this idea in our hearts will we open the path to achieving peace.

Within this broad landscape of possible actions, where does our individual responsibility lie? Human beings are political. We are concerned about society, and therefore, we cannot help but be interested in politics, as politics is the management of the masses. We also know that human beings are social, and we cannot be apart from the group. The close relationships that develop in human society are inevitable, as are the politics that grow out of these relationships. Therefore, no one in society can entirely divorce themselves from politics. The typical Buddhist attitude is to show concern with national or international affairs, but not to interfere in governance. Still, though Buddhism may transcend politics on some level, this does not mean that Buddhists lose their enthusiasm for caring about society as a whole.

Politics involves the implementation and supervising of societal affairs. Buddhists concerned with their nation's affairs might serve as a legislator or make recommendations, but not serve as a police chief, mayor, or governor who directly participates in political administration. Current social conditions across the globe are chaotic, and the standard for what is right and wrong is in disarray. I would not endorse the candidacy of monastics as national representatives in government, but I would recommend that devout members of the laity stand for election. We always need people to concern themselves with reform and the affairs of the state.

However, this is not the case for Buddhism around the world. Dr. Ananda Guruge, the former dean of academic affairs for the University of the West, was a Sri Lankan citizen who served as his country's ambassador to the United Nations. On one occasion I asked him, "What is the current relationship between Sri Lankan Buddhism and politics?" Dr. Guruge replied, "Sri Lanka has more than two hundred members of parliament, nine of whom are monastics – and excellent members of parliament I might add!"

Religion cannot separate itself from the country, nor separate itself from politics. Monastics need not hold office or manage political affairs, but they must concern themselves with society. The success of a nation is the responsibility of every citizen. And regardless of our position in society, we must not be indifferent.

The generations of eminent monastics are not like emperors and ministers who take direct charge of the government, but their love of country is the same as that of most people. They purify people's hearts and reform social mores by employing the Buddhist teachings. They supply society with mental fortifications and spiritual armor and give comfort to all who need encouragement in times of trouble and lost hope.

Some people, especially non-Buddhists, might have little knowledge regarding the concern for politics on the part of Buddhist monastics. They might hold the stereotypical notion that they cannot become involved in or concern themselves with politics. In fact, since politics involves everyone and as Buddhists care about society, why shouldn't they care about politics? Even the Buddha, himself, once said that he was "one among the group." Avalokitesvara Bodhisattva traveled to many lands by employing his thirty-two transformations, and among these were kings, ministers, and great generals. For the sake of living beings, the bodhisattva used such political backgrounds as tools to help build a pure land in this world.

Buddhists' participation in politics is based upon love of home and country as well as compassion for all living beings, and is realized by embracing the mind of wisdom. As long as Buddhists ground themselves in the spirit of compassion and aim to liberate others from pain and suffering, their participation in the business of politics will lead to the expansion of tolerance and prosperity for all.

Therefore, Buddhism cannot remain aloof from the concerns of society, the protection of human rights, or the welfare of the masses. It cannot hold to some sense of moral superiority by divorcing itself from politics. The Buddhist policy of demonstrating concern for national or international affairs, but not interfering with its governance means that an individual can be free of any craving for power and influence but not abandon the responsibility to care about society and serve the masses. To spread the Dharma for the benefit of living beings, Buddhist followers should eschew a passive attitude of avoidance, and show active concern by following through with their responsibilities as local and global citizens.

Yet as we take up these roles, we need to demonstrate through our actions that living in this human world does not necessarily require a strength to subdue others. The use of loving-kindness and service can, indeed, instill trust in others. If every country becomes more considerate of other countries and strives to be more helpful, communicative, respectful, and tolerant, then I believe we could win true peace.

We must find ways to bring differing sides closer. A family with two brothers may become embroiled in a dispute as they fight over the family's property. Yet, if someone outside the family were to attempt to cheat them, the brothers would join together to deal with that person. Additionally, even people living in a small community will not see things from a common perspective. But when attacked from an external force, everyone will pull together to resist the aggression. So must we wait for an invasion by space aliens before we can unite and create peace in this world?

Buddhism speaks of the Dharma realms as one family, and as described within the *Flower Adornment Sutra*, a single phenomenon becomes all phenomena and all phenomena arise from a single phenomenon. Everything exists within a state of interdependence, perfectly integrated in an endless, unobstructed web of existence. When viewed in this way, aren't all living things vitally connected to one another? If we could view the world as a global village and realize that we are all one family, when disaster strikes, be it aggression, an international health crisis, or an earthquake, we would all pull together to care for and help each other. This is the practice of the bodhisattva path of Humanistic Buddhism.

Chapter Twelve

On Nature:
The Way of Environmental Protection

The twenty-first century is said to be the century of environmental protection. It is easy to see why. Environmental pollution and the resulting ecological destruction now pose serious, if not irreversible, threats to the health of humankind and all living beings. Global awareness has been growing, though public outcries are often considered extremist and fall upon deaf ears. The United Nation's "Earth Summit" has met every ten years since 1992 to highlight and garner international support for conservation and environmental protection, and the message is clear. Addressing the challenge of doing our part to protect the environment to give future generations a fair chance to exist in peace and happiness on a healthy planet must become the primary ethical and scientific concern for those living in this century.

Buddhism has quite a lot to say on this topic as a religion that has always embodied the ethics of environmental awareness and protection. The Buddhist sutras, the sacred teachings compiled as far back as 2,500 years ago, implore us not only to love our neighbors, but also to love our environment. They teach us that all living beings have Buddha nature, and that every being possesses the same inherent, perfect wisdom. One story tells of a bodhisattva who loved the environment so much that he worried about polluting the earth every time he discarded a piece of paper. He worried about startling the planet every time he uttered a phrase and about scarring the ground every time he took a step. This bodhisattva's deep, vigilant mindfulness imparts a valuable example to emulate.

Unfortunately, in my adopted country of Taiwan, thoughtless acts of environmental destruction abound, such as deforestation, the dumping of toxic trash, the venting of harmful exhaust fumes into the air, and the discarding of waste-water wherever it seems convenient. These acts contribute to air pollution, water pollution, and general ecological degradation and reflect shortsightedness and a disregard for the public welfare. Other countries, such as Australia and New Zealand, for example, are much farther along in implementing measures to protect the environment. They have achieved great success in cleaning up their rivers, and their waterways are once again sparkling.

The sutras give us a wonderful example of an alternative to a world of ecological demise—Amitabha's Western Pure Land. This is a land of great beauty, and we can learn much about environmental protection from Amitabha Buddha. The sutras tell us that in the Western Pure Land, the ground is covered with gold and exquisite pagodas rise high into the sky. The land is unspoiled and the atmosphere is serene. There is no pollution of any kind. Toxins, violence, and nuclear threats are absent. The Western Pure Land is a place that many Buddhists aspire to enter upon leaving this life.

But we do not have to wait until that time comes. We can create a pure land right here on Earth. Yes, much progress is being made to protect and develop our external environment, but the important work actually lies within each of our hearts and minds. We will succeed in protecting the world's environment only when we nurture a healthy, spiritual environment within ourselves.

The Buddhist view of environmental protection is grounded in the law of dependent origination. When the Buddha attained enlightenment under the bodhi tree, he realized that all things arise because of interdependency. Nagarjuna, a great second century Buddhist commentator and scholar, explains in the *Middle Way Treatise*, "There were never any phenomena that did not arise from conditions." This means that nothing in the universe can exist independently, and all phenomena arise because of the culmination of various causes and conditions.

We know from the *Agama Sutras* that the Buddha taught about the importance of planting of trees to create shade for others, as well as to gain merit. Section Five of the *Origins of the Vinaya Sutra* also says that the Buddha stated, "A monk who plants three kinds of trees in honor of the Triple Gem—a fruit tree, a flowering tree, and a leafy tree—cultivates blessings and is not committing wrongdoing." Planting trees not only beautifies the environment, but also is a form of practice. Throughout history, Buddhist temples and monasteries have followed the Buddha's teachings by planting trees, growing flowers, and caring for our great earth.

People often regard the Buddhist religion as advocating conservatism and passivity. Many think that Buddhism primarily teaches people to recite mantras and be vegetarians. They do not associate the religion with progressive ideas such as environmental protection. In reality, Buddhism has a long history of environmental activism, developing well before the concept became popular as a social cause.

Over the past 2,500 years, Buddhist teachings have had a profoundly positive impact on the environment. Monastics have mindfully used and cared for natural resources by helping to plant trees, dredge rivers, and repair roads and bridges. Additionally, they have long maintained a tradition of encouraging others to free captured animals, thus promoting vegetarianism, and reminding all to value the gifts of nature. From these actions, we see further examples of monastics' activism, a tradition of nurturing the natural world that continues today.

These examples are well documented, but there have been many similar efforts that have escaped recognition. In their travels, many monastics throughout history have forged paths through the jungles and laid steps over jagged mountains in an attempt to ease the passage for future travelers. Without any fanfare, they have worked to balance the needs of the environment with those of sentient beings, practicing the bodhisattva spirit of providing convenience for all.

Fo Guang Shan's worldwide lay service organization, Buddha's Light International Association (BLIA), has long recognized the connection between the internal, spiritual environment and the external, natural environment and has made protecting the environment a high priority. The 1992, annual BLIA General Conference included a workshop to promote awareness of environmental and spiritual protection. As a direct result of this conference, during the following summer and in cooperation with the government of Taiwan, BLIA conducted water conservation activities. Their goal was to help preserve the water source of the city of Kaohsiung by campaigning for the planting of new trees and the preserving of existing ones. By planting new trees—two million to be exact—the water source of Kaohsiung was protected. Additionally, by advocating for the recycling of paper, the need to cut down trees was reduced, further protecting the water source.

BLIA continues this emphasis, as noted in the theme "Environmental and Spiritual Preservation" for the 2010 General Conference and in the ongoing volunteer activities of local chapters worldwide.

When we talk about protecting the environment, we should first realize there are two facets to the issue: cultivating inner peace and preserving outer, ecological balance. The former takes place on an individual level, the latter on a communal level. Each of us is solely responsible for our own inner peace. To achieve inner peace, we have to purify our own greed, anger, and ignorance. Successful efforts toward environmental protection, such as natural habitat preservation, air purification, water source cleanup, noise pollution control, trash management, and radiation protection depend upon the joint efforts of everyone.

To foster a healthy, thriving planet, we must maintain the outer, ecological balance. This can happen in two fundamental ways, by treasuring life and conserving resources. In fact, the first of Buddhism's five precepts, to refrain from killing, instructs us to treasure life. The *Brahma Net Sutra* guides us to think in this way:

> "When a follower of the Buddha exercises compassion and refrains from killing, he should think, 'All males are my fathers. All females are my mothers. Rebirth after rebirth, they give me life. All beings in the six realms of existence are my parents. Killing animals for meat is the same as killing my parents, and is, therefore, indirectly killing the source of my body.'"

The precept to refrain from killing is the expression of respect for all sentient life. To take this a step further, we should actively work to save life and help those in need. When we see an injured animal, we should care for it so that the animal can feel safe again. We need to have a proactive, compassionate, and protective attitude toward animals and be ever-mindful of our choices. For example, people often maintain exotic tastes and do not hesitate to eat anything that moves, regardless of whether it flies in the sky, moves on the earth, or swims

114 of Where Is the Way?

in the water. This type of indiscriminate slaughter and consumption not only defiles our inner spirit but also disturbs the outer balance of our natural environment and increases the violent energy in the world. To improve the quality of all life we should follow the example of the Buddha and promote the protection of all living beings.

In the *Miscellaneous Treasures Sutra* there is a story of a novice monk who was able to extend his life because of his kindness. The novice monk's teacher was a great cultivator, and had developed the power to see into the karma of others. By using his powers he was able to see that his student, due to the student's past karma, would die in the next few days.

"It has been a long time since you have seen your family," the teacher noted. "Why don't you return home to visit them?" The novice monk took his teacher's suggestion and went to see his family. Surprisingly, several days later the novice returned. "What did you do over the last week?" the teacher asked. "Nothing important. I only visited my family." "Think about it more closely," the teacher insisted. The novice monk then recalled one peculiar situation: "While journeying home I did see a group of ants trapped in a puddle of water. I placed a leaf near the puddle so they could climb out, but did nothing more." The teacher then explained the significance of sending the novice monk home. He revealed that due to the student's kind act of saving the ant's lives, the student's life was extended, and he would live to a ripe old age.

Such stories serve as reminders for us to act with compassion. Protecting life is a basic, moral principle of being human and the best tool for transforming anger, violence, and sadness into equanimity and peace. This is the message of the Buddha.

In addition to nurturing and protecting animal life, we must also treasure plant life. Even a blade of grass is vital because it works to purify the air we breathe. We must not neglect any life as each contributes to the delicate balance of which we are all a part. When we save a tree, we are making the world a little bit greener, so that all may breathe easier. Protecting life also means that we must be protective of non-sentient things, such as mountains, rivers and even everyday household items. A table, chair, or towel should be treated respectfully, because if we do not take proper care of these things and they wear out quickly, we are indirectly wasting and harming the life of these resources. The Buddha teaches us to be mindful of everything we use.

Resource conservation is crucial to environmental protection. In daily life, it is so easy to be wasteful. Consider paper for example. Trees are crucial to the environment and to our survival. They provide us with oxygen, shade, and play a key role in the water cycle. A tree that takes ten years to grow can be chopped down in a matter of minutes, yet for every ton of paper recycled, we can save twenty trees. We can also save trees by using both sides of a sheet of paper. Reducing and reusing resources represents two examples of ways that every individual can work to protect the environment.

Conservation yields benefits not only to the environment but also to us directly. Our personal resources in life, including wealth, depend upon our past actions or karma. Karma can be compared to a bank account. You have to first make deposits and accumulate some savings before you can make a withdrawal. Conservation mindfulness allows us to build up our good karma. In this regard, I can speak from personal experience.

Many devotees have complimented me on my intelligence. I believe that my intelligence is a result of my past acts of conservation. When I was a young novice monk, I was very frugal with my writing paper. On each piece of paper that I used, I not only wrote on both sides but also in between the lines. Sometimes I even used a different ink color to write over existing text, so that I did not waste paper. It was only after I could no longer decipher my own writing that I reluctantly threw away the sheet. I believe that the good karma I accrued by making the most of each piece of paper brought me the gift of intelligence. Each of us can begin to amass a stockpile of good karma by taking care of the gifts that nature gives us.

To save our earth, we must reduce the consumption of natural resources by reusing and recycling products. Including the above examples, there are many actions that require a minimum of effort. Instead of using disposable paper plates and plastic utensils, we can use reusable ones. Plastic is also not environmentally friendly, because most types are non-biodegradable and remain in landfills for decades. Polystyrene foam products are known to emit carcinogenic gases when burned. We can recycle some of these same products, such as paper, aluminum cans, plastic bottles, and many glass items. By practicing these methods, we practice the teachings of the Buddha, strengthen the connections among people, and help to spread environmental awareness.

Yet, in addition to protecting the physical environment we also need to take great care of our internal, spiritual environment. The *Vimalakirti Sutra* says, "If one wants to be in a pure land, one should purify the mind. When the mind is pure, the land is pure." This means that the environment we live in is a reflection of our state of mind. Therefore, to be successful in the effort to improve the environment, we must not neglect our inner landscape. From time without beginning, our pure nature has been defiled by greed, anger, jealousy, and malice. We must work to transform greed into generosity, anger into compassion, jealousy into tolerance, and malice into respect. When we change the way we think and the way we see the world, what we see, hear, and touch will take on a different quality.

We should also care for our body and mind like we care for the physical environment. After all, our body can be compared to the great earth. Our circulatory system is like a river, flowing ceaselessly to transport nutrients to various parts of the body. Our lungs are like forests in reverse. They take in oxygen and breathe out carbon dioxide. Our bones are like mountains, providing a protective frame for our many delicate organs. Our cells are like little, forest animals, moving about with vitality. Our being is also like a small town with six inhabitants: eyes, ears, nose, tongue, body, and mind. The mind is like the town's mayor, directing and influencing the other inhabitants. If we want good physical health, we should start with our mental health. When we have inner stability, then our body will know peace.

How do we keep our internal environment pollution free? We do so by holding the Buddha in our heart. If we have the Buddha in our heart, everything we see in the world will be the sight of the Buddha. If we have the Buddha in our heart, everything we hear will be the sound of the Buddha. If we have the Buddha in our heart, everything we say will be the word of the Buddha. If we have the Buddha in our heart, everything we do will reflect the compassion of the Buddha. In order to purify the soil and rivers of our outer environment, we must work to purify our inner, spiritual environment. This is what it means to have the Buddha in our heart. Just like a pure lotus that rises out of the muddy mire of a pond, we, too, can rise above the turbidity of the world to blossom with pristine compassion in the sun of Buddha's wise smile.

PART IV

Moving Forward on the Dharma Journey

*Each one of us is the artist of
our own life*

and can paint our own life-world;

*each one of us is the engineer of
our own life*

and can shape our own fine image.

— *Humble Table, Wise Fair*
Inspirtation

Chapter Thirteen

On the Triple Gem Ceremony: The Way of Becoming a Buddhist

Many believe that fame and fortune embody the greatest advantages in life. We chase after the wealth, the glamor, the fun that is always "over there." Yet how can we seek happiness in shifting sand? At some point, even the wealthiest, most well-established among us need to find shelter from a storm, solace in the wisdom of a teacher, and the comfort of community. And in truth, all of the advantages in the world pale in comparison to those gained by taking refuge in the Triple Gem and upholding the five precepts.

Taking refuge is the first, formal step onto the Buddhist path and signifies that we believe in Buddhism and have become disciples. The Buddha, the Dharma, and the Sangha—referred to as the Triple Gem or the Three Jewels—are the focus of faith for every Buddhist and considered the noble wealth that transcends all worldly forms. The Buddha is like the sunlight that nurtures and perfects living beings, for the Buddha is the teacher of this world;

the Dharma is like the water that nourishes living beings, for the Dharma is the truth of life; and the Sangha is like the fertile field that yields food for living beings, for the Sangha is the community of spiritual friends that sustain the Dharma. The importance of the Triple Gem is comparable to the sunlight, water and soil, without which no life could survive. Likewise, the seed of wisdom is planted through taking refuge. Thus nurtured and inspired by our confidence in the Three Jewels our practice deepens, enabling us to elevate our spiritual mind and transcend the confines of mundane life.

When a Buddhist practitioner decides to take refuge, it represents a stronger life commitment to learn, practice, and embody the virtues of the Buddha, the Dharma, and the Sangha. And taking refuge affords us limitless and immeasurable merit. Still, it is quite common to express some hesitation and doubt before requesting to take refuge. "Am I qualified?" is a question frequently asked. However, there is no need to worry. Taking refuge in the Triple Gem can only offer a multitude of benefits without doing any harm. Taking refuge is about establishing our own faith. In the event that you change your mind for some reason and no longer believe in Buddhism or even end up converting to another religion, no negative karma will result.

Whether you simply want to know about taking refuge, are exploring the idea of taking refuge, or are about to take part in the Triple Gem Refuge ceremony, you might have additional questions. In this chapter, I will address some common issues and provide a clear explanation of the meaning and significance of taking refuge in the Triple Gem, explaining how the Buddha, the Dharma, and the Sangha can be a refuge in your everyday life.

Some Answers to Basic Questions about Taking Refuge

1. Why take refuge in the Triple Gem?

To officially become a Buddhist, a practitioner must undergo the Triple Gem Refuge ceremony. When we take refuge, we devoutly make a mind-to-mind connection with the Buddha, who imparts to our mind and body the power of loving-kindness and compassion. Only after this spiritual connection has been made can we be considered a Buddhist. If we have not undergone this ceremony, but merely worship and burn incense, we are someone who honors Buddhism, but we cannot truly be considered Buddhist.

We all understand that if we want to join a political party but have yet to make the pledge, we are not an official member. Serving in a public office, such as the president of a country, also requires taking an oath of office before formally assuming the post. A new US citizen takes a formal pledge during the final citizenship ceremony. Taking refuge is similar because it formalizes and acknowledges one's commitment to the Buddha's path.

2. Do I need to become a vegetarian after taking refuge?

Taking refuge in the Triple Gem and becoming a Buddhist does not require a commitment to vegetarianism. Vegetarianism is a lifestyle and a moral question, while taking refuge in the Triple Gem is a confirmation of faith unrelated to vegetarianism. However striving to reduce the taking of life is an important spiritual practice.

3. After taking refuge, can I participate in other religious practices?

Those who take refuge can still participate in other religious practices, like honoring ancestors or paying respect at non-Buddhist temples. Taking refuge reflects a lifetime commitment, while being respectful is a momentary act. Regarding ancestors or the deities of other religions, we should be respectful. But these observances do not equate to the commitment of taking refuge. That being said, after taking refuge we should be committed to seeking the truth, and be wary of superstition.

4. Is taking refuge in the Triple Gem temporary?

Again, taking refuge in the Triple Gem is not a fleeting moment of respect; it is a lifelong commitment. According to the *Yogacara Precepts*, a day without taking refuge is a day without following the precepts. Buddhist practitioners should renew their commitment to the Triple Gem daily. By doing this, we deepen our own belief and plant the seeds that can grow into bodhi.

5. Does taking refuge in the Triple Gem mean that we worship the monastic who presided over the refuge ceremony?

Taking refuge does not mean that we worship the refuge master, but it does mean that we pay homage to the Buddha, learn the Dharma, and respect the Sangha. There are some Buddhists who may call themselves disciples of the Triple Gem, but have only taken Refuge in one. For example, they may pay homage to the Buddha, but they do not learn the Dharma or show respect to the Sangha. There are even those who only treat the Buddha as a god to whom they pray for blessings and good fortune. These people are not true Buddhist practitioners. True Buddhist practitioners not only show respect to all three gems, but also treat all members of the sangha as their teachers, study the sutras, learn the Dharma, and be close to Dharma friends. This is the true disciple of the Triple Gem.

6. After taking refuge, what is meant by living by the Triple Gem?

Taking refuge in the Triple Gem is not constrained by rules and commandments. However, our actions will manifest some changes.

For example, constantly think to yourself: "I am a Buddhist now, I will reflect and be consciously aware. I will act Buddha-like and be compassionate. I will join in Buddhist activities, support Buddhist projects," and so on. Aside from these things, those of us who take refuge in the Triple Gem will strive to develop right view and right thought. We will strive to understand and rely deeply on the law of cause and effect, and we will strive to avoid doing anything unwholesome and perform all that is wholesome. In this way, we are certain to experience the enjoyment of the Dharma and obtain the benefits of faith.

7. *What is the connection between taking refuge and the root temple?*

After taking refuge with the Fo Guang Shan Buddhist Order, Fo Guang Shan becomes the Dharma home for your life of wisdom. But you most certainly may go to other Buddhist temples to worship the Buddha. Although Buddhist temples are different, the Buddha is one and the same. Regardless of where you go, there is no need to make any distinctions.

No matter where we take refuge, whether at Fo Guang Shan or another temple, there are certainly differences between temples and sangha communities in terms of lineage. For example, if we take refuge at a Fo Guang Shan temple, it becomes the root Dharma community for your refuge. Fo Guang Shan belongs to the Dharma lineage of the Linji School of Buddhism. Everyone taking refuge through Fo Guang Shan can afterward visit other temples and participate in their activities with joy. But remember that Fo Guang Shan will always be your root Dharma home where you requested and were certified as taking the Triple Gem Refuge.

Though Buddhism is not constrained by rules and commandments, our actions will manifest some changes after taking refuge.

For example, in our individual practice, we diligently remind ourselves: "I am a Buddhist now. I will reflect and be consciously aware. I will act Buddha-like and be compassionate. I will join in Buddhist activities and support Buddhist projects." In addition, after taking refuge we will strive to develop right knowledge and view, understanding, rely deeply on the law of cause and effect, and avoid doing anything unwholesome. In this way we are certain to experience the enjoyment of the Dharma and obtain the benefits of faith.

The Meaning of Taking Refuge

The Significance of Taking Refuge

Human life cannot exist without faith, and taking refuge in the Triple Gem opens the gate to this path. Taking refuge enables our life to become more enriched, as well as more confident and peaceful. The word "gem" can refer to mundane wealth or it can refer to supramundane wealth. Mundane wealth is represented by gold, diamonds, pearls, and so forth. Supramundane wealth is represented by the Buddha, the Dharma, and the Sangha. The possession of material wealth can enrich our material life, while obtaining the supramundane wealth of the Buddha, the Dharma, and the Sangha enriches our spiritual life.

Taking refuge means that we return to and rely on the Triple Gem, for protection and to attain liberation from suffering. Children rely on their parents for protection and safety. Many seniors rely on a cane to walk more steadily. Sailors rely on instruments so they can return home safely. Likewise, the Triple Gem acts like a compass that can guide us through the great ocean of life toward a safe harbor. Therefore, taking the Triple Gem provides us a haven where we can settle down in peace within this present world, and a home to which we can always return.

Defining the Triple Gem

The Triple Gem is the collective term for the Buddha, the Dharma, and the Sangha.

Buddha is a Sanskrit word for "awakened one." It refers to a being who has awakened to the truth of the universe and has vowed to teach other sentient beings the truth, liberating them with infinite compassion. Due to his self-awakening, awakening to others, and the perfection of his enlightenment and practice, he has attained unsurpassed, perfect enlightenment, and is therefore called "the Buddha." We refer, here, to Sakyamuni Buddha, the original teacher and founder of Buddhism. But the term may also include all of the Buddhas of the ten directions and the three time periods—past, present, and future.

Dharma, another Sanskrit word, also has many meanings. The Dharma we are speaking about in this context refers to the teachings of Sakyamuni Buddha. Usually, it refers to all of the written teachings contained in the *Tripitaka*, the Buddhist canon. If sentient beings rely on the Dharma to cultivate, they will realize the truth and attain liberation.

Sangha is a Sanskrit term which translates as harmonious community. Here it refers to the monastic order whose members practice the Dharma and live together in harmony. This harmony takes on two aspects, "harmony in principle" and "harmony in action." The former means that all monastics realize the same truth about the afflictions to be removed and the truth to be realized, while the latter means that the monastics' physical, verbal, and mental actions comply with the six points of reverent harmony.

The harmonies of "in principle" and "in action," represent both the liberation of self and the liberation of others. Here, Sangha refers to the initial five bhiksus who followed the Buddha, as well as the

1,250 great bhiksus and arhats. But especially in the West, it may also refer broadly to the present Buddhist monastic order and the greater community of monastics and laity.

Ultimately speaking, the term Buddha refers to ourselves because everyone possesses a Buddha nature. In taking refuge in the Buddha, we are taking refuge in our own Buddha nature. What is called Dharma constitutes the truth. In taking refuge in the Dharma, we are taking refuge in the Dharma nature of self-awakening within each of us, as well as the undying life of wisdom. What is called Sangha represents the field of merit. In taking refuge in the Sangha, we are taking refuge in the clear field of our mind, where we can plant the seeds of compassion and merit. In this way, we can develop unwavering faith in our own merit.

To put it simply, the Triple Gem means taking refuge in the Buddha as founder, the Dharma as truth, and the Sangha as mentor. Together, they constitute the causes and conditions that enable sentient beings to attain liberation. This is why the scriptures give the analogy of the Buddha as a good physician, the Dharma as profound medicine, and the Sangha as nurses. Those suffering from illness can only find a cure when in possession of all three. Human life is just like this, for it is only by relying on the power of the Triple Gem that we can end suffering, enjoy happiness, and reach the realm of liberation.

The Benefits of Taking Refuge in the Triple Gem

Taking refuge in the Triple Gem enables us to recognize our intrinsic nature and to mine the gem-like treasury within our minds. This is because taking refuge in the Buddha means that the Buddha is the one who fully experiences truth in the human world and can guide us toward its light. Taking refuge in the Dharma can set the standard for our moral conduct. Relying upon it, we can gain right knowledge and by applying it in our practice, we can reach the shore of enlightenment. Taking refuge in the Sangha is the equivalent of having teachers who can serve as spiritual friends who, through the Dharma, guide everyone in diligent learning and practice. Drawing near to them enables us to purify our body and mind and to elevate our spiritual nature.

Taking refuge in the Triple Gem not only shows us the path to liberation, but also presents us with benefits in this present life. These include:

1. *We will become disciples of the Buddha.* By taking refuge, we accept the greatest sage of all, Sakyamuni Buddha, as our teacher, and we formally become disciples.

2. *We will not fall into the lower realms.* As the scriptures state, when we take refuge in the Buddha, we will not fall into the hell realm. When we take refuge in the Dharma, we will not fall into the animal realm. When we take refuge in the Sangha, we will not fall into the hungry ghost realm. By taking refuge in the Triple Gem, we can escape the lower realms and will only be reborn in the human or heavenly realms.

3. *We will ennoble our character.* When we don beautiful clothing, our appearance becomes more elegant. After taking refuge in the Triple Gem, our faith deepens and our character becomes more dignified.

4. *We will be supported and protected by the Dharma guardians.* The Buddha instructed the Dharma guardians and all good deities to protect the disciples of the Triple Gem.

5. *We will gain the respect of others.* After taking refuge in the Triple Gem, we will receive respect from other people and from heavenly beings.

6. *We will accomplish good deeds.* By relying on the strength and support of the Triple Gem, we will lessen our negative karma and gain peace and joy. We will then be able to achieve many good deeds in our lives.

7. *We will accumulate merit and virtue.* According to the sutras, all the merit and virtue from making offerings cannot compare with the merit of taking refuge. We can see that the benefits of taking refuge in the Triple Gem are vast and supreme.

8. *We will meet good people.* Taking refuge reduces the afflictions we experience and enables us to encounter good people as friends. No matter where we go, we will find assistance and make good connections.

9. *We will lay the foundation for taking precepts.* Only after taking refuge in the Triple Gem are we qualified to take the five precepts and the bodhisattva precepts for laypeople.

10. *We can achieve Buddhahood.* All who take refuge in the Triple Gem, even if they do not cultivate well in this lifetime, will be liberated when Maitreya Bodhisattva comes to this world because of their faith and good karmic conditions.

The Different Kinds of Triple Gem

There are classifications for the Triple Gem. The most common further divides the Triple Gem into three levels:

1. *Initial Triple Gem.* This refers to Sakyamuni Buddha, who attained the great awakening and continues to liberate others. The Initial Gem of the Dharma refers to the Four Noble Truths, the twelve links of dependent origi-

nation, and the three Dharma seals, which the Buddha taught after he attained awakening. The Initial Gem of the Sangha refers to the Buddha's first five disciples.

2. *Ever-Abiding Triple Gem.* This refers to everything that upholds the Buddha's teachings after his final nirvana: all the images of the Buddha, all written sutras, and all monastics that have ever existed.

3. *Intrinsic Triple Gem.* All people possess Buddha nature; this is the Intrinsic Buddha Gem. All people possess Dharma nature that is equal and without differentiation; this is the Intrinsic Dharma Gem. And all people possess a character that loves purity and harmony. This is the Intrinsic Sangha Gem.

The act of taking refuge in the Triple Gem is the external force through which we are guided to recognize the true self, affirm the true self, further rely on the true self, actualize the true self, and finally find the Intrinsic Triple Gem within ourselves.

Self, Other, and the Triple Gem

Everyone's Buddha nature becomes stronger after taking refuge in the Triple Gem. And given that we are all able to attain Buddhahood, what else is there that we cannot do? We just need to find the courage to carry our vows and intentions all the way to the other shore. Before taking refuge, we consider ourselves ordinary. Afterward, we recognize ourselves as the Buddha in that we can be the same as the Buddha. Therefore, every time a human being takes the Triple Gem Refuge, there are that many more Buddhas in the world.

But not yet having achieved liberation, we must also develop faith in the law of cause and effect, believe in the Dharma as a part of daily life, and maintain a solid spiritual practice. Taking refuge is nothing more than availing ourselves of another power that can guide us toward the recognition and affirmation of the Buddha nature that is within our own minds.

Yet the Chan School stresses, "Do not attach to seeking the Buddha, do not attach to seeking the Dharma, and do not attach to seeking the Sangha. You should seek nothing." This reflects the concern that we will seek the Dharma outside of the mind and will, therefore, be unable to shoulder our responsibilities. Thus, the real refuge is represented by taking refuge in the Intrinsic Triple Gem.

Our Intrinsic Triple Gem remains unchanging for all time and remains fresh and accessible across myriad eons. The Triple Gem gives us unsurpassed merit and is designated as precious gem because it retains the following six significant characteristics.

The Triple Gem is:

1. *Rare.* Living beings who lack wholesome karma will not meet with it even in a billion eons.
2. *Free of defilement.* It is free of ignorance, delusion, and contamination. It is the purest and brightest of all.
3. *Powerful.* It is endowed with awe-inspiring spiritual power.
4. *Dignifying.* It possesses immeasurable, pure merit that can dignify the supramundane world.
5. *Most supreme.* It is the supramundane Dharma, representing what is most supremely excellent and unsurpassed.
6. *Immutable.* It remains unaffected by the eight winds of praise, blame, defamation, honor, gain, loss, pain, and pleasure.

Democracy of the Mind

Let us now consider the meaning of the Triple Gem Refuge in the context of Humanistic Buddhism. As the first step along the Buddhist path, it reflects how Buddhism and the idea of modern democracy reach across the vast span of time.

In Buddhism, by taking refuge in the Triple Gem, we assert that all living beings on earth possess Buddha nature—everybody is Buddha. In taking refuge in the Triple Gem, we all occupy an equal position regardless of our ethnic origin, nationality, or religion. We all possess the intrinsic Buddha nature which is such a wonderful example of the equality of democracy.

In this way, Buddhism is similar to modern politics in a democracy where the people rule. Anyone can become president, and that person is chosen by the people in a general election. In Buddhism, anyone can become a Buddha. Therefore, not only is Buddhism adapting to the times, it is also transcending them. It has taken thousands of years for the world to slowly advance to the modern age of democracy. But the Triple Gem and the five precepts promoted by the Buddha expressed the spirit of freedom and democracy more than 2,500 years ago. And by relying upon the faith born of taking refuge in the Triple Gem, each of us can be elevated to a oneness and equality with the Buddha.

We must apply the Dharma as the standard for our physical and mental conduct after taking refuge. Be resolute in faith and transformative in moral character. This happens when we transform past greed into joyous giving, hatred into compassion, laziness into perseverance and courage, and pessimism into optimism. Then, take the next step by requesting to undertake the five precepts, the eight precepts retreat, and so on, that pertain to the laity, in order to elevate your faith to a higher level and plant bodhi seeds for enlightenment.

After taking refuge in the Triple Gem, we must work hard to protect and nurture these beginnings of the faith just like we watch over new seedlings. Maintaining a consistent practice helps us to develop our wisdom, and wisdom helps us to further affirm our Buddha nature. Most of all, taking refuge in the Triple Gem is taking refuge in our own hopes of fulfilling the potential of our wonderful human life.

Chapter Fourteen

On the Five Precepts:
The Way of Beginning the Path

Life is full of options, and the three doors of karma—body, speech, and mind—are ever present. Our choices are our life and our current life instructs our future. Day by day, moment by moment we create what comes next.

By taking the precepts, we put our beliefs into practice. They are the root of all good things and the basis for all moral conduct. When we follow the precepts, it is like students following the rules of their school or citizens abiding by the law. The difference is, that rules and laws are external forces that regulate our behavior through an outside authority, while the Buddhist precepts inspire the inner force of self-regulation or self-discipline. Without the guiding star of the precepts and our commitment to upholding them, we may continually make mistakes and bring misfortune to ourselves and to those around us.

This most fundamental set of Buddhist precepts or rules of moral conduct, observed by lay and monastics alike are to refrain from killing, to refrain from stealing, to refrain from sexual misconduct, to refrain from lying, and to refrain from consuming intoxicants.

The *Connected Discourses* tells us that not only it is important to stay away from these actions but also to fully uphold the precepts by not wishing to commit them.

The entire Buddhist moral code has evolved out of the spirit of the five precepts—the spirit of not violating others. For example, the ten wholesome acts represent an expansion and strengthening of the five precepts: to refrain from killing, to refrain from stealing, to refrain from sexual misconduct, to refrain from lying, to refrain from harsh speech, to refrain from flattery, to refrain from duplicitous speech, to refrain from greed, to refrain from anger, and to refrain from ignorance. And though the precepts in Buddhism are divided into different sets of monastic precepts and lay precepts, the five precepts constitute the basis of them all and are known as the fundamental precepts of Buddhism. They symbolize the entrance to the Buddhist path.

A Few Relevant Issues

The Five Precepts and Freedom

Many of us think that after taking the precepts, life becomes a matter of you-can't-do-this and you-can't-do-that. We worry that life in this way will mean a loss of freedom. Therefore some people also ask, "Why should I take the precepts and end up just limiting myself?"

If we conducted a survey at a prison to investigate the reasons for the prisoner's incarceration, we would find that every, single inmate had violated one or more of the five precepts. Murder and aggravated assault that maims someone constitute violations of the precept against taking life. Graft, embezzlement, stealing, extortion, robbery, and kidnapping are violations of the precept against stealing. Rape, prostitution, sexual abuse, human trafficking, and lewd behavior are violations of the precept against sexual misconduct. Defamation, breach of promise, false accusations, false testimony, rumor mongering, planting evidence, and threats of violence represent violations of the precept against lying. Drug dealing, drug usage, and drug trafficking represent violations of the precept against consuming intoxicants. And this is, by no means, an exhaustive list.

The point is we can easily find ourselves in jail with our freedom revoked because we violated the five precepts. Thus, observing the precepts assures us that we are following the laws of society. Only those who are able to take, uphold, and truly understand the precepts will enjoy real freedom. The true meaning of the precepts is freedom, not limitation.

The Five Precepts and Vegetarianism

Becoming vegetarian is not a requirement after undertaking the five precepts. Just as in the case of taking refuge in the Triple Gem, there are no special dietary restrictions. Still, the Buddhist faith is all about helping us to become more compassionate, more moral, and to value and protect life.

The Dharma gives us the optional practices of observing the three kinds of clean flesh and only eating the vegetables of a meat dish. In this context, "clean flesh" refers to the meat of any animal that we have not seen killed, have not heard being killed, and meat that has not been killed for us personally. We can also observe the six vegetarian fast days every month and daily vegetarian breakfasts. In these ways, we can work toward the self-purification of our body and mind in order to become a more compassionate and moral practitioner.

The Five Precepts and Karmic Retribution

Since Buddhism teaches about karmic retribution, people often conclude that if we eat the meat of pigs, horses, cows, or sheep, we will receive the future retribution of being reborn as those animals. If we swat a fly or squash an ant, we will be reborn as a fly or an ant. Following this logic, if we kill a human being, we would be reborn as a human being. However, as rebirth in the human realm is a rarity resulting from our past, positive karma, such views demonstrate a misunderstanding of karmic retribution. These wrong views actually place us in a worse situation than breaking a precept. Breaking a precept is a transgression, an error that can be corrected through repentance. When we hold wrong views, we are cut off from the Buddhist path.

In Buddhism, there is nothing shameful about breaking the precepts, for as long as we sincerely repent, we can still be hopeful about life. But holding a wrong view is similar to having an incurable disease that no medicine can treat. The same can be said for those in politics, for the commission of errors in thinking is quite serious. In terms of the Buddhist moral code, mistaken thinking and understanding are like the five kinds of views that cloud the meaning of karma. The five kinds of views include views of the body, extreme views, evil views, views that attach to wrong views as truth, and views attached to immorality. All are sources of affliction and obstruct us on the Path. Thus, when we follow Buddhist teachings, we need first to develop right knowledge and understanding. We need not fear the precepts, for it is only through them that we can enjoy peace, security, and protection.

The Five Precepts and Repentance

If we break the precepts after taking them, what can we do? Sometimes people think that since we will be unable to avoid breaking them, it might be easier if we do not take the precepts at all. Then we would not have to worry about breaking them. Actually, the negative karma from breaking the precepts lessens when we have a sense of regret and repentance. In this way, we still have a chance to obtain liberation. If we do not take the precepts and commit harm without any sense of remorse, then our negative karma is all the more severe as we do not see a reason to correct our behavior.

The Five Precepts and the Benefits of the Buddhist Moral Code

The benefits of taking and upholding the five precepts, the Buddhist moral code, constitute the basis for human morality. According to the *Empowerment Sutra*, in taking and upholding the five precepts, we are sure to acquire the protection of twenty-five Dharma guardians. The *Moon Lamp Samadhi Sutra* also says that those who uphold the precepts with a pure mind will gain ten benefits.

1. They will have the fulfillment of all wisdom.
2. They will learn what the Buddha learned.
3. They will become wise, and not be slandered by others.
4. Their bodhi mind will not regress.
5. They will be settled in the state of cultivation.
6. They will be free from the cycle of birth and death.
7. They will be able to admire the tranquility of nirvana.
8. They will have an undefiled mind.
9. They will attain Samadhi.
10. They will not experience a lack of faith or Dharma wealth.

We must not only take and uphold the five precepts in a passive manner, but also actively by going a step further in our behavior. Not only must we refrain from killing, we must also protect life; not only must we refrain from stealing, we must also practice generosity, not only must we refrain from sexual misconduct, we must also give respect; not only must we refrain from lying, we must give true words; and not only must we refrain from consuming intoxicants, we must act correctly. In upholding the precepts we can eliminate our suffering, afflictions, and fear in this lifetime, and gain the freedom, peace, harmony, and joy of body and mind, while showing compassion to others.

Upholding the Five Precepts

After taking and observing the five precepts, should we then try undertaking some other Buddhist precepts? Upholding the five precepts is a lifetime undertaking, not something one does for only twenty-four hours. The five precepts can be taken and upheld all at once or in stages. We can select the one or two precepts that are the easiest to observe according to our own situation, and then practice more diligently with three or four until we gradually reach the full five precepts. We can go even further by aspiring to take the higher level bodhisattva precepts, consisting of the ten major and forty-eight minor precepts.

Generating the bodhi mind for enlightenment in order to accomplish the work of enlightenment will ensure that our ventures will be more successful and our family life more fulfilling the mundane world. Our spiritual life will also become more expansive in the supramundane world. Roaming the dharma realm freely and peacefully is truly the finest state of human life.

The Five Precepts Explained

The precepts are the basis upon which unsurpassed enlightened Buddhahood is accomplished. They constitute the foundation for the threefold training of morality, meditative concentration, and wisdom. Therefore, the first step when we follow Buddhism is to take refuge, after which we take the next step by taking and upholding the Buddhist moral code of rules and precepts.

The First Precept Is to Refrain from Killing

To refrain from killing, broadly speaking, is about not violating or harming others. Any taking of life is considered killing, from grave offenses such as killing a human being, to less serious instances such as killing ants or mice. However, Buddhism is a religion that emphasizes human beings, so this precept most specifically refers to refraining from killing human beings.

A common question that arises about taking the five precepts concerns unintentional killing, such as accidentally hitting a mosquito or a fly or smashing an ant during the course of daily life. With respect to the Buddhist moral code, the two categories of taking life are *duskrta*, minor misdeeds, and *parajika*, grave offenses. Parajika means beyond redemption, something that cannot be remedied through repentance. Only the taking of human life constitutes the grave offense of parajika. Killing cockroaches, ants, and the like is considered an act of wrongdoing and will still carry with it negative karmic effects. But it is not on the same level as killing a human being.

Other things like wasting time or squandering material resources can also be considered killing. Because life is the accumulation of time, when we waste time, we are taking away life. Material resources belong to all beings and require the effort of sentient beings to bring about the right conditions for their existence. Therefore, when we casually destroy these resources, we also take away life. The foremost purpose of this precept is to encourage us to nurture our compassion.

The Second Precept Is to Refrain from Stealing

To refrain from stealing is to avoid taking the property of others. To put it simply, when we take things that do not belong to us without permission, it is stealing. Additionally, taking what is not given includes taking things that are left unattended or having others take something for you. Engaging in such activities as shoplifting, political corruption, embezzlement, misappropriation of funds, unfair or illegal business practices, gambling, and prostitution operations all break with the Buddhist moral code.

Even if we take paper, envelopes, pens, or other supplies from our workplace, or if we borrow things and do not return them, we are engaging in impure conduct. Although they do not break a fundamental precept, we will still be held responsible and have to suffer the negative karmic effects. Therefore, it pays to be mindful!

The Third Precept Is to Refrain from Sexual Misconduct

Sexual misconduct is sexual behavior that violates the law or the rights of others. For example, rape, prostitution, pedophilia, sexual slavery, adultery, and other sexual acts that harm and negatively affect our society are all violations of this precept. As a further example, unrequited love often makes our thoughts unclear, and we become disturbed by our desires and anxieties. This causes us to lose peace of mind and possibly causes others harm. Since the purpose of upholding the precepts is to purify the body and mind, this kind of behavior is contrary to that purpose.

Sexual misconduct is a fuse that ignites chaos in society. For example, the problems of incest and child prostitution disgrace all of civilization. If people would uphold the precept of refraining from sexual misconduct, these situations would not occur. If all couples resolved to uphold this precept, families would be more harmonious and society more peaceful.

The Fourth Precept Is to Refrain from Lying

Speech karma comprises four of the ten unwholesome acts. Lying includes divisive speech, duplicitous speech, flattery, and telling untruths. Lying refers to, for example, seeing something and saying that you did not, not seeing something and saying you did, or calling what is right wrong and calling what is wrong right. Lying is also spreading rumors to cause trouble, telling tales to create discord, ruining the reputation of others, and spoiling the good works of other people. We need only a single sentence to actually cause others to suffer enormous pain.

Lying has many different levels as well, such as bearing false witness with evil intent and harming others through irresponsible and casual remarks. We should also consider as lying the telling of a white lie and anything else that causes harm.

The Fifth Precept Is to Refrain from Consuming Intoxicants

Not consuming intoxicants refers to not taking substances that dull the senses, and cause us to lose self-control and violate the morals of society. Alcohol, marijuana, opium, amphetamines, glue, and cocaine are just a few of the many examples. However, when the Buddha established this precept, it applied specifically to alcohol.

In the first four precepts, the essential nature of the behaviors that we must refrain from involves immorality. The essential nature of drinking alcohol is not itself immoral, but it can cause people to lose self-control and engage in killing, stealing, lying, and sexual misconduct.

According to the *Great Compendium of the Abhidharma Treatise*, there was once a layperson who, after getting drunk, stole his neighbor's chicken and broke the precept against stealing. He then killed and cooked the chicken, violating the precept against killing. When his neighbor's wife asked about it, he lied and said that he had not seen the chicken, breaking the precept against lying. At this time he noticed the beauty of the neighbor's wife, so he raped her and violated the precept against sexual misconduct.

From this story, we can see that when people drink too much or use other intoxicants, they may lose their sense of shame, remorse, and self-control. They may commit any of the four serious crimes of killing, stealing, lying, and sexual misconduct. Therefore, in order to avoid causing harm to others or to ourselves, it is best to uphold this precept and abstain from consuming intoxicants.

The Five Precepts in Summation

The five precepts are the major, fundamental precepts of Buddhism, and taking and upholding them are not only direct causes for entering the Buddhist path, but also the best medicine for purifying the mind.

Buddhism fosters the act of giving and Buddhists cultivate this practice. This practice promotes using things outside of the body as a way of benefiting others, and only those with a disposition for charitable donations are able to achieve altruism. Taking and upholding the five precepts and adhering to the ten wholesome acts constitute means to employ moral conduct and achieve purity of mind. We can then bring peace and respect to others, enabling everyone to take care of each other, and to enjoy the greatest freedom. This is the merit of not violating others, something far greater than that accrued from charitable giving.

Freedom of the Mind

In taking and upholding five precepts, the spirit of the precepts is freedom. This is so because when we uphold the precepts, we will not violate others, and as long as we can discipline ourselves, we will also not break the laws of society. The restraints of the law will not weigh upon us, and we will be able to enjoy a free and independent life. Transgressing the five precepts is not only prohibited for those who follow the Buddha's path, but also are not permitted or condoned under the laws of secular states. Therefore, if everyone strictly upheld the five precepts, we would, surely, have a more caring and joyful world.

Chapter Fifteen

On Buddhism and Democratic Principles:
The Way of Equality

We all understand democracy as a political entity, a form of government ideally characterized by freedom, equality, and government by the people. But how many of us have considered any similarities between democracy and Buddhist principles? In this chapter, I want to explore these connections in order to illustrate that Buddhism has much to offer as we progress further into the era of the global village.

Taking refuge in the Triple Gem—which means taking refuge in the Buddha, the Dharma, the Sangha and the Buddha nature that all people and the Buddha possess—expresses the equality that lies at the heart of democracy. Upholding the five precepts, respecting others, and not willfully violating someone else's rights, represent the true meaning of freedom. And tolerance is a must for any of us to survive in today's world. Only through the wisdom of tolerance and compassion will we see our way through the suffering that surrounds us, whether as nations or as individuals.

Therefore, looking more closely at these two concepts and their relationship with democracy will not only bring us more in touch with the Buddha's message given to his first disciples over 2,500 years ago, but also enable us to see the benefit of his teachings in our own present moment.

Taking Refuge in the Triple Gem and the Spirit of Democracy

Why do we say that taking refuge in the Triple Gem is the manifestation of democracy? The answer lies in the Buddha's earliest teachings. He taught his disciples that "all sentient beings possess Buddha nature; all can become Buddhas." Simply put, every sentient being is a future Buddha, and all Buddhas were once sentient beings. Therefore, taking refuge in the Triple Gem means taking refuge in ourselves, in our own beautiful potential to overcome suffering.

As future Buddhas, these insights and abilities are as true for us as they are for the Buddha, hence the expression: "There is no difference between the mind, the Buddha, and sentient beings." The Buddha elevated all sentient beings to a spiritual level equal to his own. Is this not democratic? By taking refuge in the Buddha, we pledge to become disciples in order to uncover the Dharmakaya within our own mind of wisdom, just as the young Prince Siddhartha did some 2,500 years ago.

We also take refuge in the Gem of the Dharma, the teachings of the Four Noble Truths that are true for all beings in the universe. This truth is our original mind, is eternal, and exists within all things. The *Vairocana Sutra* states, "No matter when all Tathagatas appear or disappear, Dharma is always abiding." The phrase "Dharma is always abiding" means that life is without end, and that sentient beings and the Buddha are alike in that we can all realize the Dharmakaya. In other words, all sentient beings possess an equal ability to realize the Dharma and to achieve liberation.

The Gem of the Sangha represents the pure, harmonious, and peaceful Buddhist community. It stands as a model for all people and heavenly beings, and serves as a bridge between them. The members of the sangha have one teacher, one path, the same views, and they abide by the same rules. They handle all business through collective opinion and strength, successfully leading a life based on the six points of reverent harmony. Fortunately for us, Buddhist history provides numerous examples of this egalitarian structure in action.

From the first assemblies that met following the Buddha's entry into final nirvana to the sanghas of today, meetings have been conducted in the spirit of democracy, with many decisions being made by consensus of all assembled. Everyone is heard; everyone is represented. In addition, the sangha is not only concerned with reaching consensus in internal meetings, but also through holding meetings of the faithful that require the four orders of bhiksu, bhiksuni, upasaka, and upasika to attend. By bequeathing such a democratic organization, the great Buddha fully demonstrated his thoughts and ideas about the nature of community.

Yet this sort of organization should not be viewed solely as an external structure. We possess the truth of the Buddha, the Dharma, and the Sangha in the same spirit as this monastic organization—within our own hearts. The sangha members are our teachers in developing the pathway of our hearts. They manifest the Dharmakaya and the Buddha nature that exists within all sentient beings. Therefore, as we learn from the sangha, so we learn from the Buddha. From their lessons, we realize that struggle, opposition, and suffering result arise from clinging to the concept of ego. From their lessons, we begin to glimpse the significance of no-self, equality, and connection as forerunners to peace and freedom in the world.

Upholding the Five Precepts and the Path to Freedom

Why do we say that upholding the five precepts means freedom? When Buddhism speaks of upholding the precepts, the meaning relates to the ultimate aim of all moral behavior. The spirit of the precepts is to prevent harm and suppress evil by not infringing upon another's rights or hindering another's freedom for the sake of our own. Only by respecting the rights of others can there be freedom. Therefore, taking the five precepts and vowing to uphold them is also the foundation of humanism.

Master Huiyuan of Mt. Lu said, "The Buddhist way of liberating people is important. Why? If ten people out of a village of one hundred families uphold the precepts, then ten people will be honest. If a hundred people out of a state of one thousand families practice the ten wholesome acts, then one hundred people will be at peace. If one spreads this teaching far and wide among a thousand households, then there will be tens of thousands of benevolent people. Practicing one virtue means eliminating one evil. Eliminating one evil means getting rid of one punishment. Once one punishment is eliminated, thousands can be eliminated throughout the country."

Therefore, by taking and upholding the five precepts, we can find relief from misery, trouble, and fear, and can recover freedom, tranquility, harmony, and happiness. Likewise, if whole societies could do the same, then the nations of the world could become a pure land. If everyone, including those of us who are leaders in our nations, could also arrive at a true understanding of cause and effect, our societies would no longer be hotbeds of trickery and deceit. If we could all embrace the compassionate spirit of Buddhism and take the five precepts, our world would lose much of its cruelty. With these insights we can see that the power of karma to produce good and bad is of our own creation. Therefore, this concept of free will in the power of karma is truly in accord with the meaning of freedom.

Advocating for Equality

History presents us with the wide variety of political forms that have existed over time, forms devised to order and explain society and human interaction. Even democracy has played out in different configurations across time and place. But the primary tenets of democracy to promote freedom and human rights remain the same. Today, people the world over are speaking out not only for freedom and equality in political representation, but also for respect for the sanctity human life.

Buddhism, too, champions the right to life, political participation, freedom, equality, and culture. But Buddhism broadens the concept of the right to life to include all sentient beings. The Buddha taught that all sentient beings possess Buddha nature; all beings have the right to life and none should consider the taking of life lightly. Therefore, these concerns for all sentient beings express the Buddhist belief in the protection of life.

Liberating sentient beings is more than simply providing food and clothing. This sort of minimal assistance is in no way sufficient to solve the sufferings of all sentient beings. What is important is the birth and death of sentient beings, their afflictions, their security, and the means to protect them. We must accept the principle that all sentient beings are equal and genuinely protect their right to life and lead them away from suffering toward happiness and achieving liberation and ease.

Vegetarianism and conservation provide us with two increasingly poignant examples. In India, most dining halls in the railway stations are vegetarian. In the United States, there are supermarkets that do not sell meat. In addition to religious principles for not consuming meat, serious health concerns also play a role, and both reasons constitute ways of protecting the right to life. In order to commiserate with and protect all sentient beings, Buddhism always advocates having great compassion, which implies vegetarianism. But in the propagation of Buddhism human beings are the focus, and owing to difference in local environments and customs, there are no great demands placed on eating and drinking. The primary goal is that we not view the taking of any life lightly.

Therefore, in the broadest sense, living beings, a grain of sand, a stone, grass, and trees are all the result of the power of the universe. Intentionally harming or reducing the lifespan of something is a kind of killing. Nature and all living things are intimately interconnected in a web of life, all of which deserve to be treasured. Unfortunately, for a long time now, humanity has ignored this precious interconnection, often killing and wasting life to satisfy a momentary whim. If we intentionally harm the environment, then one day when the consequences manifest and humankind finds itself buried in landslides, swept away by floods, assailed by dust storms, and suffering from the depletion of the ozone layer, the results of cause and effect will be something fearful.

Equality is the only proper course to initiate peace, and there will be peace only when there is equality. Peace and equality are two sides of the same truth. When we say that all sentient beings are equal, we mean that from the Buddha to sentient beings, all are honored with life and have the right to life. Only when the right to life is advocated and when all life in the universe is seen as one, will there be equality. Only when there is equality will there be democracy. And only when there is democracy will there be freedom. So within the realm of relationships and governance, we find even more strands of the web that is life on this planet.

Gathering Insight

Several years ago, I lectured on taking refuge in the Triple Gem, taking the five precepts, and the issue of the right to life. I believe that by taking refuge in the Buddha, we can light a lamp in our hearts, like building a power plant. By taking refuge in the Dharma, we can open a spring in our hearts, like building an oasis of compassion. And by taking refuge in the Sangha, we can open a field within our hearts in which to sow the five grains of moral behavior, establishing a spiritual home of our own and leading a happy life.

When it comes to taking and upholding the five precepts, there is really only one: Do not harm others or ourselves. This encapsulation of the precepts represents the true meaning of freedom, which is to protect our own freedom without depriving others of their own. If we are to build a global village of democracy and peace, we need to rid ourselves of distinctions, inflexibility, and doing harm to others. If we can see ourselves and others as one, enemies will not exist. If we can respect and forgive one another, where will peace not be found?

Democracy is the wave of today, an ideal to be cherished and promoted. From a Buddhist perspective, freedom is a right that all people are born with, a right that generates equality and the potential for peaceful coexistence. With these insights, I hope that in the future, all people can reach this consensus and cooperate with one mind to create a radiant world of the Buddha's light of democracy, freedom, and equality.

Chapter Sixteen

On the Future:
The Way of Development

The saddest thing in life is when a person has no hope for the future. People thrive on hope. People have children to make provisions for old age. They raise and educate them hoping that they will be successful. Strengthening family ties and living in harmony with neighbors implies the hope that we can all live together peacefully in the future. Planting trees and flowers and storing grain in the event of famine also exhibit a sense of boundless hope. Even today's organ transplants are a hope to extend life.

People willingly pay taxes with the hope that the nation will improve in the future. Bridges and roads are repaired in the hope that transportation will become more convenient. Public assistance is provided with the hope of keeping poverty at bay. The capable and wise are elected with the hope that government will become increasingly more democratic. Punishing corrupt officials is done with the hope that government will become more ethical. Everyone today hopes that there will be good weather for crops, that their country will be prosperous, that people will live in peace, and that the world will soon know peace. Hope is the future of humankind and our planet.

Buddhism, too, not only values the past but also the future, because the future is our hope. The taking of vows provides the perfect example. Many Buddhists vow to be reborn in a pure land where they will learn to serve all sentient beings. During the refuge ceremony, new devotees vow to take refuge in the Buddha, the Dharma, and the Sangha, and all Buddhists hope to attain enlightenment. Those who give alms, form good affinities, and transfer merit all do so with the hope that things will be better in the future. With just these few examples we can see that in Buddhism as in the rest of the world, the concepts of hope and the future are intertwined in our lives.

Children learn how to behave from their parents with the hope of becoming successful, well-adjusted adults. In school, a child acquires knowledge in the hope of a good future. People work during the day and put in overtime in the evening in the hope of a better tomorrow. Animals hibernate to survive harsh winters and hopefully will awaken to freshness and plenty in the spring. Ants and bees also store food for the future. Plants become dormant in the winter, yet their roots remain alive so that life might spring anew in the future.

The future demonstrates the continuity of life, an unending river forever flowing. And though the span of our current life is brief, it returns to the boundless future. Therefore, it can be said that a person who lives a day will make plans for the next hundred years. This is a beautiful hope.

Science makes astounding advances to improve the future of human beings, and philosophers propose ideals to enrich human thought. Writers create perfect futures to tweak and inspire our imaginations. Industrialists design and produce to improve the lot of humanity. Many revolutionaries sacrificed themselves for their hopes for the future. And despite the dangers, despite the setbacks, humanity continues to struggle for the future, filling it with boundless hope, promise, and beauty.

The future of humanity, war, economics, biology, and space are universal topics of study. And it is safe to say that all scholars are looking to the future. We are already planning long-term occupation of outer space. Biologists are studying ways of extending human life and repairing genes. Geographers are leading people to open up wastelands and deserts. All of this is possible, fostered by those thinking of the betterment of humankind and fueled by burgeoning advances in information technology.

When we look at the *Amitabha Sutra*, we read that the Western Pure Land is paved with gold, the water runs hot and cold, and the birdsong and sound of flowing waters speak the Dharma. In the Western Pure Land, there are no traffic jams, there is no lust, and thoughts and sights are filled with joy. Long ago, Buddhism depicted a beautiful future where everything is as we could wish it. This is the Western Pure Land of Amitabha Buddha.

From a Buddhist perspective, a society pervaded by the Buddha's light would be a pure land of our world, with a government dedicated to the protection of all life, and a religion of truth. The pure land spoken of by Buddhism is not just the Western Pure Land of Amitabha Buddha, the Pure Land of the Medicine Buddha, or the millions other Buddha lands. The pure land of Buddhism is something that can be made manifest in the world today. As the *Vimalakirti Sutra* states, "Where the mind is pure, the land is pure." This means that although the world is dirty, chaotic, unstable, and filled with afflictions, it is just an expression or our imperfect minds. If our minds achieve perfection, then the future will shine with the Buddha's light and never again have political, class or gender conflicts. There will be no haves and have-nots, and life will be free from worry. There will be no troublemakers or governmental oppression. Society will be stable and happy. Thus, the Western Pure Land can be realized before our very eyes, and our world can become a pure land.

A pure land in this world is the ideal society for the future. If we strictly adhere to the five precepts, practice the four means of embracing and the six perfections, fully understand cause and effect and the Noble Eightfold Path, it will not be difficult to realize. The span of human life stretches from the past to the present and into the future. The road of life lasts just a few decades, but birth leads to death and death to rebirth, time and time again into the future, affording us myriad opportunities for the creation of a pure land.

But what does the future hold? What will it be like? If we look at the Buddhist concepts of the three time periods and cause and effect, we can gain some insight. The present exists because of the past, and the future will exist because of the present. The purpose here is not to get stuck in one or the other, but to understand how one time period informs the other. The concept of the three time periods is, therefore, vital as the area of future studies involves making predictions using what is known about the past and the present.

In Buddhist thought, the law of karma and the law of cause and effect speak to our roles as the architects of our own futures. Therefore, if we really want to know the future, we can simply take hold of it! The *Cause and Effect of the Three Time Periods Sutra* asserts, "If you want to understand your present, look to the past for causes. If you want to know effects in the next life, they are to be made in this life." In other words, any cause will produce a similar effect. All people are free to decide their own life's path.

But we cannot rest in the present and be complacent, because without taking the next step, how can we arrive at the future? If there is no hope, no ideals to reach for, why talk about goals or achievements? Knowing that there is the possibility for happiness in the future makes current suffering easier to bear. And if we can learn from the past, understand the power of the present, and envision the potential of the future, we will perceive the three time periods through a lens of wisdom and compassionate energy, insuring a brighter and more complete life.

Although the ultimate aim of Buddhism is the pursuit of nirvana and spiritual liberation, we exist within the moments our worldly lives. The Dharma advocates "first entering the world in order to leave it." Hence, "seek the Dharma and enlightenment in this world, for seeking wisdom apart from this world is like looking for horns on a rabbit." In other words, we are born into this world and cannot live apart from it.

Moving through the days, most of us live a material life, a life of complex emotions, a collective life as social animals, and a life oriented through our bodily senses. These are the ways in which we generally navigate the world, find our place, and of course, attempt happiness. Buddhism defines this basic existence as mundane Dharma.

Yet, we should remember that all life is characterized by impermanence and delusion. Consequently, each of these aspects of worldly life possesses its own caveat that we would do well to heed. Material things are limited, and our boundless desires can never be satisfied. For these reasons, we should live sensible, economical lives. Emotions will not leave us satisfied forever. Therefore, we should attempt to purify them. Collective life, though beneficial, entails inevitable conflict. We should, therefore, live according to the six points of reverent harmony. And lastly, our bodily senses lead to consciousness and perceptions that change with each moment due to causes and conditions. Therefore, we should live a life of faith and joy in the Dharma.

Yes, there are caveats to our worldly existence. But as you can also see, Humanistic Buddhism provides suggestions to help us rise above the mundane, a blueprint for life that enables us to move forward on the journey toward liberation and hope. And this blueprint is absolutely necessary for the realization of a Humanistic pure land in our world. The section of the *Vimalakirti Sutra* entitled "The Buddha Way," offers a further summation of Humanistic Buddhism:

> Wisdom is the mother of all bodhisattvas,
> Skillful means the father;
> All guides and teachers
> Are born of such parents.

> Joy in the Dharma is their spouse,
> Compassion is their daughter,
> Goodness and sincerity their sons;
> Home is the contemplation of emptiness.

> Worldly affairs are their disciples,
> Transformed at will.
> Dharma is their good friend
> Through which enlightenment is attained.

> The six perfections are their companions,
> The four means of embracing their musicians;
> The words of the Dharma
> Are their music and song.

> Their garden is planted with
> The trees of no outflows,
> The flowers of enlightenment,
> The fruit of the wisdom of liberation.

Their pool of eight liberations
Is filled with the water of concentration,
Planted with the lotuses of the seven purities;
It is where the pure bathe.

The five supernatural powers are their draft
    animals,
Their vehicle the Mahayana,
Their driver one mind,
Their road the Noble Eightfold Path.

Their appearances are solemn,
Their ornaments auspicious,
Their clothing good conscience,
Their garlands virtuous aspiration.

Their wealth is the seven kinds of Dharma treasure,
And their teachings enrich others;
All their speech and cultivation
Are dedicated to the great benefit.

Their bed is the four meditations,
Where the pure way of life is born;
Their enlightenment comes from
Constantly learning and increasing wisdom.

Their food is the sweet dew of the teachings,
Their drink the juice of liberation;
Their bath is the pure mind,
The precepts their perfume.

Having conquered all afflictions,
They are invincible.
Having subdued the four maras,
They raise their standards on the field of enlightenment.

They are willingly born
Though they know of no arising or extinction.
They appear in all the Buddha realms
Like an omnipresent sun above.

Though they worship the countless Buddhas
In the ten directions,
They never dwell on the slightest difference
Between themselves and the Buddhas.

The proof of Humanistic Buddhist theory lies in the Buddhist scriptures. The Buddha's teachings are filled with humanism, and Humanistic Buddhism was, in fact, the Buddha's original concern. Therefore, it can be said that two and a half millennia ago, the Buddha had already fully drawn up the Humanistic Buddhism blueprint for life for the sake of all sentient beings. The question up until now has been how to propagate Humanistic Buddhism and help others to realize the blueprint. This is what all followers of the Buddha should diligently work toward.

I do not think that Humanistic Buddhism can simply remain on a conceptual level but must be actively realized. For this reason, over the last fifty years Fo Guang Shan has steadfastly maintained Humanistic Buddhism's four objectives of propagating the Dharma through culture, nurturing talent through education, benefiting society through charity, and purifying people's minds through cultivation.

In the area of culture, in addition to editing the Buddhist canon, *Fo Guang Dictionary* was completed in 1989, providing an immense resource for Buddhists at home and abroad. The *Chinese Buddhist Sutra Series* translates the scriptures into modern vernacular for clarity of comprehension in the world today. Fifteen years ago, I organized a group of about one hundred people to compile the *Essential Guides to Buddhism* and the *Fo Guang Textbooks* for use as systematic introductions to Buddhism.

In 2000, Fo Guang Shan founded the *Merit Times* newspaper, and edited the *Universal Gate Buddhist Journal*, the *Chinese Buddhist Academic Series*, and the *Chinese Buddhist Cultural Essays*, a series of books to encourage research on Buddhism. Beautiful Life Television now provides visual channels of communication for Buddhism and a way to transmit the Dharma to all on a daily basis. Cultural enterprises such as the Gandha Samudra Cultural Company, the Fo Guang Cultural Enterprise, and the Oracle Records Company, publish periodicals for laypersons and scholars alike. In these ways, media are being utilized to propagate the Dharma and benefit sentient beings worldwide.

In the area of education, in addition to founding sixteen Buddhist academies, five universities, twenty-six libraries, and over twenty art galleries to develop talent, we have held Buddhist examinations to further promote the study of Buddhism around the world. Local branch temples also hold summer camps, Buddhist conferences, urban Buddhist academies, and Sunday schools for children to sow the seeds of wisdom in all corners of the globe.

In the area of charity, the Great Compassion Children's Home, the Charitable Medical Corps, and numerous retirement homes and cemeteries have been established to meet the diversity of needs. In addition, throughout the world volunteers of the branch Fo Guang Shan temples devote much time to caring for their communities through service projects.

Finally, regarding the area of teaching and practice, Fo Guang Shan holds an Amitabha chanting service at the same time every Saturday throughout the world. And in response to local needs, regularly scheduled practice sessions in meditation halls, recitation halls, and ceremonial halls provide people with invaluable opportunities to purify their minds.

In my own life, I have done my utmost to promote Humanistic Buddhism. When I lecture on the sutras, I want everyone to understand. When I write articles, I want them to be accessible to everyone. In establishing temples, I want people to be able to use them. In organizing activities, I want everyone to be able to attend. In organizing Dharma services, I want everyone to experience the joy of the Dharma, and in propagating Buddhism internationally, I insist upon providing translation resources. I try to meet the needs of the people, whatever the time and place. This is because the Buddhism that people need is practical Buddhism.

In 1954, in order to meet the demands of the time and the needs of sentient beings, I proposed the printing of hand-bound Buddhist books and teaching on the streets. Gradually, I spread Buddhism to jails and schools and spoke on radio and television. I also organized Taiwan's first Buddhist choir to help spread the teachings throughout the island. Over the last sixty years, I have diligently turned the temples into lecture halls and textbooks into Buddhist reading materials. I have taken individual practice and made it collective. I have made the recitation of sutras into lectures on sutras. And in order to involve lay followers in the propagation of Buddhism, I established Buddha's Light International Association and a lecturer system in the hope that the Humanistic Buddhism blueprint for life could gradually be realized under the radiating light of the Buddha.

All of these successes demonstrate that regardless of how good the Dharma is, it must meet the needs of society and benefit the people if it is to be of value. Promoting Humanistic Buddhism really means to engage people in the practice. It has to be more than mere slogans. And the whole point of practice is to encourage us to move further along the bodhisattva path. We want to help ourselves and others to find the joy that flows from the Dharma, the wealth of heart that blossoms from compassion, and the immeasurable peace that arises as we uncover our own Buddha nature.

Humanistic Buddhism is the future of mainstream Buddhism. This is the inevitable and hopeful trend of the times because Humanistic Buddhism is the Buddhism needed by people.

Conclusion

Living Our Vows:
The Way of Happiness

So here we are. As in the cycle of life, we find ourselves at the ending of one journey while on the threshold of another. The information and knowledge presented in this book are stepping stones to realization and insight that could lead to the making or reaffirmation of vows and the commitment to living those vows:

> Sentient beings are limitless; I vow to liberate them.
> Afflictions are endless; I vow to eradicate them.
> Teachings are infinite; I vow to learn them.
> Buddhahood is supreme; I vow to attain it.

Therefore, with each moment there is rebirth. With each breath there is new opportunity. And with each vow we can experience the continual unfolding of our Buddha nature.

The founder of Buddhism, Sakyamuni Buddha, was born into this world. He cultivated himself in this world, attained awakening in this world, and shared with others the deep truths he

realized in this world. The human world was emphasized in everything he did.

Why did the Buddha attain awakening as a human being and
not as a heavenly being, an asura, an animal, a ghost, or in hell?
Taking this question one step further, why did the Buddha not
attain awakening in the distant future or the forgotten past? Why
did he choose our world and our time? There can only be one reason:
the Buddha wanted the teachings of Buddhism to be relevant to the
human world.

The Buddha's life as a human being can serve as an inspiration
and a model for spiritual practice in our own lives. We call the teachings of the Buddha Humanistic Buddhism to emphasize that they
can be integrated into all aspects of our daily lives, the means of
which are outlined in six characteristics.

1. *Humanity.* The Buddha did not come or go without leaving
   a trace, nor was he some sort of illusion. The Buddha
   was a living human being. Just like the rest of us, he had
   parents, a family, and he lived a life. It was through this
   human life that he showed his great loving-kindness and
   compassion, his moral character, and his wisdom.

2. *Emphasis on daily life.* The Buddha taught that we must
   practice his teachings in our daily lives. He provided guidance on everything, from how to eat, dress, work, and live,
   how to walk, stand, sit, and sleep. He gave clear directions
   on every aspect of life from how to maintain our relationships with family and friends to how we should conduct
   ourselves in the social and political arenas.

3. *Altruism.* The Buddha was born into this world to teach,
   to provide an example, and to bring joy to all beings. He
   nurtured all beings, for he always had the best interests

of others in his mind. In short, his every thought, word, and action arose from a deep care and concern for others.

4. *Joyfulness.* The Buddhist teachings give people joy. Through the limitless compassion of his heart, the Buddha aimed to relieve the suffering of all beings so that they could be happy.

5. *Timeliness.* The Buddha arose in this world for one great reason: to build a special relationship with all of us who live in this world. Although the Buddha lived some 2,500 years ago and has already entered final nirvana, he left the seed of liberation for all subsequent generations. Even today, the Buddha's ideals and teachings serve as timely, relevant guides for us all.

6. *Universality.* The Buddha's entire life can be characterized by his spirit of wanting to liberate all beings, without exclusion. The Buddha loved beings of all forms, whether they were animals or humans, male or female, young or old, Buddhist or non-Buddhist. He cared for all without distinction.

As we can see from these characteristics, Buddhism is a religion for all people, and human concerns are at its heart. Throughout the Buddhist sutras, the Buddha emphasized that he, too, was part of the sangha to emphasize that he was not a god. The *Vimalakirti Sutra* states, "The Buddha realm is found among sentient beings. Apart from sentient beings, there is no Buddha. Apart from the assembly, one cannot find the Way." Huineng, the Sixth Patriarch of the Chinese Chan School said, "The Dharma is within the world. Apart from the world there is no awakening." To become Buddhas, we must train and cultivate ourselves in the world. There is simply no other way. Now that we have been fortunate enough to be reborn as human beings, we should integrate our practice of Buddhism into our daily lives.

We should also not take our life for granted. By way of explanation, the *Connected Discourses* draws the following analogy: Imagine that there is a blind sea turtle in a vast ocean. Floating on top of the vast ocean is a wooden ring, just big enough for the tortoise to poke his head through. If the turtle only comes up for air once every one hundred years, the likelihood that he will poke his head through the ring is greater than the chance of being reborn as a human being. The *Agama Sutra* also say, "The number of beings who lose their human birth are as numerous as the particles of dust on the earth. The comparative number of those who are able to gain a human birth are as scarce as the dirt under a fingernail." This story illustrates how rare and precious human life is.

Once I attended a Buddhist study group at the home of a devotee in San Francisco. A teacher in the group said to me, "When you ask us lay Buddhists to work toward freeing ourselves from the wheel of rebirth, we have no such desire. When you teach us the path to Buddhahood, we have no such aspiration. Both of these are too remote and distant. We just want to know how to live our lives a little better than others, a bit more cultivated than others?"

His words worried me, because many people view Buddhism as a religion removed from humanity. They see an isolated Buddhism, a Buddhism of monastics surviving only in the mountains and forests, and a self-centered Buddhism. For them, Buddhism has lost its human quality. It has reached the point where many who are interested in learning more about Buddhism dare not do so. They hesitate as they peer in and wander about outside. We must redouble our efforts to affirm that Buddhism is invested in the liberation of all sentient beings, and can provide meaning and benefit to everyone. We want to demonstrate that we can bring Buddhism home to our daily lives.

The history of Buddhism is characterized by the rise, development, and evolution of many schools of thought and practice, including the Theravada, Mahayana, and Vajrayana schools. While each school carries its own rich interpretation of the Buddha's teachings, Humanistic Buddhism represents an integration of all Buddhist teachings from the time of the Buddha. And regardless of tradition, Buddhism should maintain its emphasis on humanity in order to remain relevant as times change. Precisely because Humanistic Buddhism attends to the trends of the current age, it can also be a beacon for the future.

Buddhism is a religion for all people, and human concerns are at its heart. China's four sacred mountains are named for their association with the four great bodhisattvas: Avalokitesvara, Manjusri, Samantabhadra, and Ksitigarbha. Of these four, Avalokitesvara, Manjusri, and Samantabhadra manifest as laypersons. Only Ksitigarbha Bodhisattva manifests as a monastic. Why? The life of a monastic emphasizes detachment from and transcendence of the mundane world, while the life of a layperson allows for the optimism and engagement in the world that can realize the goals of Mahayana Buddhism. Master Taixu once said, "I am not a bhiksu, nor am I a Buddha. Rather, I wish to be known as a bodhisattva." Master Taixu dared not call himself a bhiksu, for it is very difficult to perfectly uphold the monastic precepts, and he also was not yet a Buddha. He saw himself as a man of great service, and thus wished to be known as a bodhisattva.

In Buddhism there is the concept of the pure land. A pure land is a realm created through the power of a Buddha's vows to ease the suffering of living beings. All people would like to live in a place such as this. Buddhists frequently mention Amitabha Buddha's Pure Land of Ultimate Bliss in the west, or the Medicine Buddha's Pure Land of Pure Crystal Radiance in the east. But there are more pure lands than just those in the east or west. Maitreya Bodhisattva, who will become this world's next Buddha, resides in the Tusita Pure

Land and the *Vimalakirti Sutra* mentions the pure land of the mind. Pure lands are everywhere.

Humanistic Buddhism seeks to create a pure land on earth. Instead of resting our hopes on being reborn in a pure land in the future, we can aspire to transform our world into a pure land of peace and bliss. Instead of committing all of our energies to some later time, we can direct our efforts toward purifying our minds and bodies right here and now, in the present moment. Humanistic Buddhism focuses on the world right now, rather than on leaving the world behind, on benefiting others rather than benefiting ourselves, and on liberating all beings.

Humanistic Buddhism recognizes that the material and spiritual aspects of life are equally important and, therefore, calls for a life that finds a balance. There is the external world of action as well as the internal world of the mind. There is the world ahead of us and the world behind us. If we always insist on charging blindly into what is ahead, we will get hurt. It is also important to look back, and to look within. As a practice, Humanistic Buddhism supports both the perception of form and emptiness, having many possessions and no possessions, and for community and solitude. By finding the Middle Way, a balance in all things, Humanistic Buddhism enables people to achieve a beautiful and fulfilling life.

I believe that desiring to serve others, giving others a helping hand, establishing friendly ties with others, and giving others joy are the teachings of the Buddha. In other words, the goal of Humanistic Buddhism is to make Buddhism relevant in our world, in our lives, and in our hearts. Simply close your eyes, and the entire universe is there, within. Even if all people in the world abandon you, your Buddha nature will never leave you.

In today's societies, we are all burdened with responsibilities. We all feel stressed from the obligations of our homes, businesses, and families. So how can we live happily and contented? By applying the Buddha's teachings to our everyday lives, the whole universe can be ours, and we can be happy and at peace in all we do. This is the spirit of Humanistic Buddhism.

GLOSSARY OF NAMES AND TERMS

Abhidharma. Sanskrit for higher doctrine. The philosophical commentary on the Buddha's teachings and the third basket of the Buddhist canon.

afflictions. Suffering born of greed, anger, and ignorance.

alaya-consciousness. Skt. *alaya-vijnana.* The eighth and most subtle level of consciousness and the level in which karmic seeds are stored. Also known as the store consciousness in the Mind-Only School.

Amitabha Buddha. The Buddha of boundless light and infinite life. Amitabha is one of the most popular Buddhas for devotion among Mahayana Buddhists. He presides over the Western Pure Land.

Ananda. One of the ten great disciples of the Buddha. Noted as the foremost in having heard much. After the Buddha entered final nirvana, Ananda is said to have recited the verbal teachings of the Buddha and compiled the sutras in a cave at Rajagraha (Rajgir), India, which is in Magadha, India, where the five hundred disciples of the Buddha were assembled.

animal realm. *See* **six realms of existence**.

anuttara samyak samhodhi. A Sanskrit term meaning complete, unexcelled awakening; an attribute of all Buddhas.

arhat. Sanskrit for worthy one. One who has attainted awakening and achieved liberation.

asceticism. Skt. *dhuta.* This means to eliminate afflictions and sufferings, to cultivate the mind and the body by sacrificing the comforts of clothing, food, housing and transportation. To abandon desires.

asura realm. *See* **six realms of existence.**

attachment. A deluded mental factor that observes a contaminated object, regards it as a cause of happiness, and wishes for it.

Avalokitesvara Bodhisattva. The bodhisattva of compassion, whose name in Sanskrit means observing the sounds of the world. He is known as one of the great bodhisattvas of Mahayana Buddhism.

Awakening. The state of awakening to the ultimate truth—freedom from all afflictions and suffering.

bhiksu. The male members of the Buddhist monastic community who have renounced household life and received full ordination. Therefore, bhiksus are known as beggars or the one who eliminate afflictions.

bhiksuni. The female members of the Buddhist monastic community who have renounced household life and received full ordination. Therefore, bhiksunis are known as beggars or the one who eliminate afflictions.

Blessed One. Skt. *Bhagavan* or *Bhagavat* in early translation, Ch. *Shizun* in later translated works. Usually translated as World Honored One in English.

bodhi. Enlightenment. Awakening to one's own Buddha nature and vowing to liberate all sentient beings.

Bodhidharma. First Patriarch of the Chinese Chan School, who brought Chan from India to China.

bodhi mind. Skt. *bodhicitta*. The mind that seeks enlightenment and vows to liberate all sentient beings.

bodhisattva. Refers to one who is seeking the attainment of Buddhahood or liberation, and one who practices all perfections. Bodhisattvas remain in the world to help others achieve enlightenment. The concept of the bodhisattva is the defining feature of Mahayana Buddhism.

bodhisattva path. Skt. *Bodhisattva-carya*. Indicates the cultivation of the bodhisattvas in Mahayana Buddhism. Main philosophy of the bodhisattva path is to attain Buddhahood and liberate all sentient beings through the practice of the six perfections.

bodhisattva precepts. Additional Mahayana precepts that focus on liberating ourselves and other living beings from suffering. Primarily drawn from the *Brahma Net Sutra*, which lists forty-eight minor precepts that should be observed as well as ten major precepts to be kept at all time.

Brahmans. Highest caste of ancient India. Typically priests and scholars. Acted as intermediaries between the gods, the world, and human beings. *See*: **caste**.

Buddha. Sanskrit for Awakened One. Though there are many Buddhas, the term typically refers to Sakyamuni Buddha, the historical Buddha and founder of Buddhism.

Buddha nature. The capacity to become a Buddha that is inherent in all living beings.

Buddhahood. The attainment and expression that characterize a Buddha and the ultimate goal of all sentient beings.

Buddha's Light International Association. BLIA. Lay Buddhist organization founded in 1992 by Venerable Master Hsing Yun. Works to promote Buddhism, education, culture, and community service. There are two hundred chapters throughout the world.

Buddhism. Founded by Sakyamuni Buddha around 2,500 years ago. Basic doctrines include the three Dharma seals, the Four Noble Truths, the Noble Eightfold Path, the twelve links of dependent origination, the six perfections, and the concepts of impermanence and emptiness. Its three, main traditions are the Mahayana, Theravada, and Vajrayana schools. While Buddhism has been a popular religion in much of Asia, it is gaining increasing popularity in the West.

caste. Category of strict social division in ancient India. The Indian caste system of the Buddha's time featured four castes: *Brahman* (priests), *Ksatriya* (warriors and kings), *Vaisya* (merchants), and *Sudra* (manual laborers). The Buddha opposed the caste system.

causes and conditions. Used to analyze causal relationships in a Buddhist context. A cause denotes the major factor which produces an effect, while a condition is a factor whose presence allows for a cause to produce a given effect.

Chan School. One of the schools of Chinese Buddhism, brought to China by Bodhidharma. It emphasizes the cultivation of intrinsic wisdom and teaches that awakening is illuminating the mind and seeing one's intrinsic nature. A major tenet of the Chan School is that the Dharma is wordlessly transmitted from mind to mind.

Confucianism. The philosophy named after Confucius (551-479 BCE), who is known as Kongzi in Chinese and was an early Chinese moral philosopher. Official philosophy of China between the third century BCE and the fall of the Qing dynasty in 1911. The philosophy of Confucius emphasized personal and government morality, corrections of social relationships, justice and sincerity.

Consciousness-Only School. Also known as Mind-Only School. One of the two, primary Mahayana schools that developed in India which asserted that all phenomena originate from consciousness. The school subsequently had major influences on Buddhist thought in China, Japan, and Tibet.

cycle of birth and death. Skt. *samsara.* Also known as transmigration. When sentient beings die, they are reborn into one of the six realms of existence, a continuous cycle due to the karmic result of one's deeds.

dependent origination. Buddhist concept that all phenomena arise due to causes and conditions. Thus, no phenomena possesses an independent self-nature. The twelve links of dependent origination are ignorance, mental formations, consciousness, name and form, the six sense organs, contact, feeling, craving, clinging, becoming, birth, and aging and death.

Devadatta. A monastic disciple and cousin of the Buddha who wished to wrest leadership of the sangha away from the Buddha. He attempted to murder the Buddha several times.

Dharma. Sanskrit for truth. Refers to the Buddha's teachings, as well as the truth of the universe. When capitalized, it denotes both the ultimate truth and the teachings of the Buddha. When the term appears in lowercase, it refers to anything that can be thought of, experienced, or named. This usage is close in meaning to the concept of phenomena.

Dharmakaya. The body of Dharma, which indicates the true nature of the Buddha or the unity of Buddha with all phenomena. Known as one of the three bodies of the Buddha: Dharmakaya, Samboghakaya, and Nirmanakaya.

Dharmodgata. Also known as Fayong, traveling monk during the Tang dynasty who practiced asceticism, made pilgrimages, and translated sutras.

eight consciousnesses. Consciousnesses of eye, ear, nose, tongue, body, mind, manas, and alaya. *See* **alaya-concsiousness**.

eight precepts. A special set of precepts that are usually taken as a retreat for one day and night for lay Buddhists to experience monastic life. They include the five precepts in addition to precepts to refrain from eating at inappropriate times, wearing perfumes and personal adornment, watching singing and dancing, and sleeping on luxurious beds.

emptiness. Skt. *sunyata*. The concept that everything in the world arises due to dependent origination and has no permanent self or substance. All phenomena are said to be empty of an inherently independent self.

enlightenment. The state of awakening to the truth. Awakening to one's intrinsic nature, freedom from all afflictions and suffering, and rebirth in the six realms of existence.

Esoteric School of Buddhism. Based upon the Vairocana Buddha's self-realized state of esoteric mystery depicted in the *Mahavairocana Sutra* and the *Susiddhikara Tantra*. It is also known as the Mantra School in Japan, since the recitation of sacred formulas called mantras is one of the school's main practices.

final nirvana. The state of having completed all merits and perfections and eliminated all unwholesomeness. Usually used to refer to the time when the Buddha physically passed away.

five aggregates. Skt. *skandhas*. Elements that make up a human being: form, feeling, perception, mental formations, and consciousness.

five contemplations. Five methods of contemplation for stopping and eliminating delusions: (1) Contemplation of the impurity of the body. This enables sentient beings to eliminate greed in the mind. (2) Contemplation of loving-kindness and compassion. This enables sentient beings to eliminate anger and hatred in the mind. (3) Contemplation of causes and conditions. This enables sentient beings to eliminate ignorance and afflictions in the mind. (4) Contemplation of a Buddha. This enables sentient beings to eliminate unwholesome thoughts and the stress of uncomfortable situations. (5) Contemplation of counting the breath. This helps sentient beings to eliminate distractions and achieve single-mindedness.

five meal contemplations. (1) Assess the amount of work involved, weigh up the origins of the food. (2) Reflect on one's own moral conduct, perfect or not, take this offering. (3) Safeguard the mind against all error, do not give rise to hatred or greed. (4) Regard this food as good medicine, so as to treat the weakened body. (5) In order to accomplish the Way, one deserves to accept this food.

five precepts. The fundamental principles of conduct and discipline that were established by the Buddha for wholesome and harmonious living: to refrain from killing, to refrain from stealing, to refrain from sexual misconduct, to refrain from lying, and to refrain from consuming intoxicants.

five vehicles. Indicates the five vehicles or paths of sentient beings in their practice toward enlightenment and Buddhahood. These include human, heaven, sravaka, pratyekabuddha, and bodhisattva.

Fo Gang Shan. The monastic order established by Venerable Master Hsing Yun in 1967 in Kaohsiung, Taiwan. The term literally means "Buddha's Light Mountain" and is used to refer to the association of over two hundred branch temples around the world, and over one thousand monastics ordained by Master Hsing Yun.

four bases of mindfulness. Skt. *smrtyupasthana.* Mindfulness of the body, feelings, thoughts and dharmas: (1) contemplate the impurities of the body, (2) contemplate the suffering of feelings, (3) contemplate the impermanence of the mind, (4) contemplate the non-selfhood of all phenomena.

four elements. Skt. *catvari mahabhutani.* In Buddhism, all matter in the world is composed of the elements of earth, water, fire, and wind.

four great kindnesses. To: (1) parents, (2) sentient beings, (3) rulers and nations, (4) the Triple Gem.

four immeasurable minds. Skt. *catvari apramanani.* (1) immeasurable loving-kindness, to give others happiness. (2) immeasurable compassion, to help others find freedom from suffering. (3) immeasurable joy, to feel joyful when others can stay away from suffering, (4) immeasurable equanimity, to treat others equally without discrimination.

four means of embracing. The four methods that bodhisattvas use to guide sentient beings to the path of liberation: (1) giving, (2) kind words, (3) altruism and beneficence, and (4) sympathy and empathy.

Four Noble Truths. A fundamental and essential teaching of Buddhism that describes (1) the presence of suffering, (2) the causes of suffering, (3) the cessation of suffering, and (4) the path leading to the cessation of suffering.

four offering verse. I make offering to the Buddha. I make offering to the Dharma. I make offering to the Sangha. I make offering to all sentient beings.

four reliances. Four guidelines for Buddhist practitioners to stay on the path: (1) rely on the Dharma, not on an individual teacher; (2) rely on wisdom, not on knowledge; (3) rely on the meaning, not on the words; and (4) rely on the ultimate truth, not on relative truth.

four right efforts. Skt. *samyak prahana*: (1) eliminate arisen unwholesomeness, (2) prevent unwholesomeness which has not yet arisen, (3) generate unarisen wholesomeness, (4) increase wholesomeness which has already arisen.

Four Universal Vows. Four vows of Mahayana Buddhism that are said to initiate the seed of bodhi mind in a practitioner if sincerely taken to heart. They are: (1) Sentient beings are limitless, I vow to liberate them; (2) Afflictions are endless, I vow to eradicate them; (3) Teachings are infinite, I vow to learn them; (4) Buddhahood is supreme, I vow to attain it.

fourfold assembly. The collective name for male Buddhist monastics; female Buddhist monastics; male lay Buddhists; and female lay Buddhists.

gatha. Verses.

heavenly realms. Buddhism describes many heavenly realms in which one can be reborn. Life in the heavenly realms is pleasurable, but impermanent, and one is still subject to the cycle of birth and death. *See* **six realms of existence**.

Huineng. The Sixth Patriarch of the Chinese Chan School of Buddhism. His teachings emphasized that enlightenment can occur suddenly, and his words were recorded as the *Platform Sutra*, one of the school's most influential texts.

Huiyuan. (334-416 CE). A student of Dao'an and the First Patriarch of Pure Land School of Buddhism in China.

human realm. *See* **six realms of existence**.

Humanistic Buddhism. Represents a return to the principles laid down by the Buddha. Emphasizes practice of the Way in daily life and building a pure land in our world. Venerable Master Hsing Yun is a proponent of Humanistic Buddhism.

hungry ghost. One mode of rebirth for those that die with a large amount of craving. *See* **six realms of existence**.

impermanence. One of the most basic truths taught by the Buddha. It is the concept that nothing in this world exists and remains forever and all conditioned phenomena will arise, abide, change, and disappear due to causes and conditions.

kalpa. An Indic unit of time measurement, a significantly long period of time. There are three types: small kalpas, medium kalpas, and large kalpas. A medium kalpa is the length of twenty small kalpas. A large kalpa is the length of four medium kalpas. A large kalpa is the length of the time that a world system undergoes a cycle of formation, abiding, destruction, and void.

karma. All wholesome and unwholesome actions, speech, and thoughts, and their effects. *See* **causes and conditions**.

King Asoka. King of the Maurya Kingdom in India from 272-236 BCE. He was the foremost royal patron of Buddhism in India and the first monarch to rule over a united India.

ksana. Buddhist term describing the smallest possible unit of time.

law of cause and effect. Skt. *heta-phata*. This is the most basic doctrine in Buddhism, which explains the formation of all relationships and connections in the world. This law means that the arising of every phenomenon is due to its own causes and conditions, and the actual form or appearance of all phenomena is the effect.

liberation. Skt. *vimoksa*. Freedom from all afflictions, sufferings, and the cycle of birth and death.

lower realms of existence. *See* **six realms of existence**.

Mahakasyapa. One of the ten great disciples of the Buddha. He is known as foremost in austerities, and is considered the First Patriarch of the Indian Chan School of Buddhism.

Mahaprajapati. Prince Siddhartha's aunt who raised him after his mother's death. She later became a female disciple of Sakyamuni Buddha. The bhiksuni order was established as a result of her requests to the Buddha.

Mahayana Buddhism. Mahayana is Sanskrit for Great Vehicle. One of the three, main traditions of Buddhism, along with Theravada and Vajrayana. It stresses that helping other sentient beings to achieve enlightenment is as important as self-liberation.

Maitreya Bodhisattva. The future Buddha of our world. He currently presides over Tusita Heaven, where he is expounding the Dharma to heavenly beings.

Manjusri Bodhisattva. The Bodhisattva of Wisdom. He has the wisdom to see the true nature of all dharmas. Typically depicted as sitting on a lion. He and Samantabhadra Bodhisattva are usually described as standing on the left and right-hand sides, respectively, of Sakyamuni Buddha.

mantra. A sound, a particular group of syllables, or words used as a concentration device or incantation formula.

mara. A malevolent being that embodies desire and is an adversary of the Buddha. The name is also used to refer to mental qualities that impede spiritual progress.

Master Taixu. He is the reformer of Chinese Buddhism in the late nineteenth and early twentieth centuries. His works are included in the set of the *Complete Works of Master Taixu*.

Master Xing'an. The Ninth Patriarch of the Pure Land School, born in the Qing dynasty.

merit. Blessings that occur because of wholesome deeds.

Middle Way. A teaching of Sakyamuni Buddha which teaches the avoidance of all extremes.

Nagarjuna. One of Buddhism's most influential philosophers, born in India in the second or third century. Founder of the Madhyamaka School and the author of many commentaries and treatises, such as the *Middle Way Treatise* and the *Great Perfection of Wisdom Treatise*.

namo. Skt. *namas*. It means to venerate or to take refuge in.

Never-Disparaging Bodhisattva. In one of his previous lives, Sakyamuni Buddha was this bodhisattva. According to chapter twenty of the *Lotus Sutra*, he was a bhiksu in the Vinirbhoga Kalpa when the Bhisma-garjitasvara Buddha preached the Dharma. He always had praise and respect for everyone, including bhiksus, bhiksunis, upasikas, and upasakas.

nirvana. A Sanskrit word that means extinction. A state of perfect tranquility that is the ultimate goal of Buddhist practice. It refers to the absolute extinction of all afflictions and desires, the state of liberation beyond birth and death.

Noble Eightfold Path. The path leading to enlightenment as taught by Sakyamuni Buddha. It includes: right view, right thought, right speech, right action, right livelihood, right effort, right mindfulness, and right meditative concentration.

no-mind. An expression which refers to the mind which is empty of discrimination and transcends the duality of existence and non-existence.

non-self. Skt. *anatman*. A basic concept in Buddhism saying that all phenomena and beings in the world have no real, permanent, and substantial self. Everything arises, abides, changes, and extinguishes based on dependent origination.

pattra-leaf sutras. Early Buddhist scriptures written on the leaves of plants.

phenomena. An English translation of dharma when it is used to refer to thoughts, sensations, and other units of reality.

prajna. It is mostly translated as wisdom. Yet it has a closer connotation of supreme awareness, cognition, and understanding. Typically refers to a transcendent variety of wisdom that comes from seeing the true nature of reality. Prajna-wisdom is considered the highest form of wisdom.

pratimoksa. A list of rules governing the behavior of all monastics. *See **Tripitaka**.*

pratyekabuddha. One who attains awakening on his or her own, without having heard the teachings of a Buddha.

pure land. A transcendent realm created through the power of a Buddha's vow to help ease the suffering of living beings, should they choose to be reborn there. One of the most commonly discussed pure lands is the "Western Pure Land of Ultimate Bliss."

Rahula. The son of Prince Siddhartha and one of the Buddha's ten great disciples. At the age of six, he entered the sangha and was instructed by Saripurta. He was considered foremost in esoteric practices.

saha world. This indicates the world where we reside, which is full of suffering. Saha means endurance, and though the world is tormented by the suffering, human beings have the power to endure it. Beings in this world endure suffering and afflictions from their greed, anger, and ignorance.

Sakyamuni Buddha. Siddartha Gautama, the historical Buddha and founder of the religion know today as Buddhism. The name Sakyamuni means sage of the Sakyans. Sakya was the name of his clan.

Samadhi. Literally, to establish or make firm. A state in which the mind is concentrated in a one-pointed focus and all mental activities are calm. In samadhi, one is free from all distractions, thereby entering a state of inner serenity.

Samantabhadra Bodhisattva. He personifies transcendental practice and vows. He typically sits on a white elephant with six tusks, symbolizing to the six perfections.

sangha. Traditionally the Buddhist monastic community. In a broader sense, the community that includes monastics and laypersons.

Sariputra. Pali: *Sariputta*. One of the Buddha's ten great disciples. He is known as the foremost in wisdom.

sentient beings. Skt. *sattvas*. All beings with consciousness, including heavenly beings, asuras, humans, animals, hungry ghosts, and hell-beings. From the Mahayana viewpoint, all sentient beings inherently have Buddha nature and therefore, possess the capacity to attain enlightenment.

six perfections. Six qualities that bodhisattvas develop on their way to Buddhahood: giving, morality, patience, diligence, meditative concentration, and wisdom.

six realms of existence. Used to describe the basic Buddhist cosmological scheme. The six realms of existence refer to possible destinations of rebirth: heaven, asura, human, animal, hungry ghost, and hell. The six realms also indicate where we reside and all the modes of existence in which forms of suffering are embodied due to greed, anger, and ignorance. When sentient beings die, they are reborn, a cycle that continues as a result of one's karmic actions.

six sense objects. The six senses of human beings: sight, sound, smell, taste, touch, and dharmas. It refers to those objects which are recognized the six sense organs of eye, ear, nose, tongue, body, and mind.

skandha. *See* **five aggregates**.

sramanera. A male novice in a Buddhist order who has vowed to uphold the ten novice precepts but has not yet received full ordination.

sramanerika. A female novice in a Buddhist order who has vowed to uphold the ten novice precepts but has not yet received full ordination.

sravaka. Literally, one who has heard. One who has been liberated from the cycle of birth and death after listening to the Buddha's teachings but does not seek to become a Buddha.

Subhuti. One of the Buddha's ten great disciples. He was foremost in understanding emptiness.

suchness. Skt. *tathata*. A term for the true nature of all things; the pure, original essence of all phenomena.

sudden enlightenment. An abrupt, immediate attaining enlightenment, often due to a skillful teaching by a master. This was a common technique expounded by the Chan School.

suffering. Skt. *dukkha*. The First Noble Truth referring to the state in which the body and mind are oppressed by afflictions.

supreme marks. The thirty-two excellent marks of the Buddha and the eighty accessory marks.

sutra. A Sanskrit word used to describe a variety of aphoristic writings for spiritual development. Most commonly used in a Buddhist context to refer to the recorded discourses of the Buddha.

Tathagata. One of the ten epithets of a Buddha. Literally translated as "Thus Come One," meaning the one who has attained full realization of suchness, true essence, or actuality. One who dwells in the absolute beyond all transitory phenomena, with the ability to freely come and go everywhere.

ten Dharma realms. Where is resided by ordinary and noble beings in Buddhism, divided into the following ten categories, progressing from the lowest to the highest: hell-beings, hungry ghosts, animals, human beings, asuras, heavenly beings, sravakas, pratyekabuddhas, bodhisattvas, and Buddha.

ten wholesome acts. No killing, no stealing, no sexual misconduct, no lying, no duplicity, no harsh words, no flattery, no greed, no anger, and no ignorance.

the Way. In Buddhist contexts, refers to the path leading to liberation taught by the Buddha.

Theravada School. One of the eighteen schools in the period of Sectarian Buddhism. In the third century BCE, it was transmitted to Sri Lanka from India. Considered one of the three, main schools of Buddhism.

three Dharma seals. Three statements of truth in Buddhism which are universally applicable to all phenomena. According to the *Connected Discourses of the Buddha* in the Chinese Buddhist cannon, they are: (1) All conditioned phenomena are impermanent, (2) All phenomena are without an independent self, and (3) Nirvana is perfect tranquility. In some Buddhist texts such as the *Dharmapada Sutra*, they are: (1) All compounded things are impermanent, (2) All compounded things are unsatisfied, and (3) All dharmas are without self.

three poisons. The root causes of all suffering: greed, anger, and ignorance.

three realms. The realms where sentient beings reside and transmigrate: (1) the desire realm, (2) the form realm, and (3) the formless realm.

three studies. Skt. *trisiksa*. Refers to morality, concentration and wisdom. Morality can prevent one from the unwholesomeness of body, speech, and mind. Meditative concentration can enable one to eliminate distracting thoughts with a singly-focused mind, see the true nature, and attain the Way. Wisdom can enable one to reveal their Buddha nature, eliminate all afflictions, and see the Truth. It is also referred as the three higher trainings.

three time periods. Refers to past, present, and future lifetimes.

three vehicles. Skt. *trini yanani.* Refers to paths to carry sentient beings to the other shore of enlightenment: the sravaka, the pratyetkabuddha, and bodhisattva.

Tiantai School of Buddhism. One of the eight major schools of Chinese Buddhism. This school was named after its founder Zhiyi, who lived on Mount Tiantai. The school derives many of its teachings from the *Lotus Sutra.*

Triple Gem. Also called the Three Jewels. Refers to the Buddha, the Dharma, and the Sangha.

upasaka. A male lay-follower of the Buddha who does not renounce the household life or enter a monastery but still strives to live a spiritually cultivated life and upholds the teachings and precepts.

upasika. A female lay-follower of the Buddha who does not renounce the householder life or enter a monastery but still strives to live a spiritually cultivated life and upholds the teachings and precepts.

Vajrayana. Also called the "Diamond Vehicle." One of the three, main schools of Buddhism.

Vinaya. The rules and regulations for Buddhist monastics.

Vulture Peak. Skt. *grdhrakuta*. Located in the northwest of the ancient city of Rajagrha in ancient Magadha Kingdom. Sakyamuni Buddha discoursed several major sutras here, including the *Lotus Sutra*. It is now a famous pilgrimage site.

Western Pure Land. Where Amitabha Buddha presides. It came into existence due to Amitabha Buddha's forty-eight great vows. Sentient beings can make a vow to be reborn there, where they can practice without obstructions.

without outflows. Skt. *anasrava*. The state of "without outflows" refers to liberation. Sometimes the term refers to those teachings that are free from afflictions and leading to liberation.

World-honored One. One of the ten epithets of the Buddha and means the most venerable of the world.

Xuanzhuang. Also known as Xuanzang. A great master in the Chinese Tang dynasty (602-664 CE). He was one of the four great translators of Buddhist teachings, studied in India for seventeen years, and was an expert on the *Tripitaka*. He was also responsible for bringing many collections of works, images, pictures, and relics to China from India. One of his most famous works is the *Buddhist Records of the Western Regions*.

Yogacara. Commonly used to refer to the Consciousness-Only School of Buddhist philosophy.

Zhaozhou. Chan master of the Tang dynasty. Also known as Zhaozhou Congren.

GLOSSARY OF SUTRAS AND TEXTS

Amitabha Sutra. One of the three sutras that form the doctrinal basis for the Pure Land School of Mahayana Buddhism.

Ascent of Maitreya Sutra. Translated into Chinese by Juqu Liangsheng in the Liu Song dynasty. One of Maitreya's three sutras and the most recent of the three.

Brahma Net Sutra. Translated into Chinese by Kumarajiva during the Latter Qin dynasty. It describes the stages of cultivation in the bodhisattva path, the ten major precepts, and the forty-eight minor precepts that should be upheld.

Chinese Buddhist Canon. Contains discourses, monastic rules, and treatises translated from the earlier *Tripitaka*. The oldest version was translated in the Chinese Han dynasty. During the Song dynasty it began to be printed and published by the official government.

Collected Essential Teachings Sutra. Translated into Chinese by Richeng during the Song dynasty.

Commentary on the Main Mahayana Doctrines. Translated by Fahu, Weijing, et al. It describes the Dharma methods of Mahayana practice and cultivation for Buddhists.

Commentary on the Middle Way Treatise. The work of Chinese Master Jiaxiang Jizang in 608 CE.

Connected Discourses. Translated into Chinese by Gunabhadra (394-468 CE). It is so named because those whom the Buddha taught included bhiksus, bhiksunis, upasakas, upasikas, and heavenly beings. The teachings also included several subjects such as the Four Noble Truths, the Noble Eightfold Path, and dependent origination.

Contemplation of the Buddha of Infinite Life Sutra. Translated into Chinese by Kalayasas during the Liu Song dynasty. It describes sixteen methods of contemplating the Western Pure Land and is one of the three sutras of the Pure Land School.

Contemplation of the Mind Sutra. Translated into Chinese by Prajna in 790. It describes the Buddha's discourse at Vulture Peak to Manjusri, Maitreya, and other great bodhisattvas on the contemplation of the mind, the elimination of delusions, and the attainment of Buddhahood.

Descent of Maitreya Sutra. Translated into Chinese by Dharmaraksa during the Western Jin dynasty. One of Maitreya's three sutras, it describes Maitreya Bodhisattva's descent from heaven to this world, his cultivation, and his attainment of Buddhahood.

Dharmapada Sutra. Also known as the *Words of Truth* or the *Treasury of the Truth.* An anthology of verses, arranged topically. It is one of the most beloved of Buddhist text in the West.

Diamond Sutra. This title refers to the insight gained through this sutra, for it is like a diamond that cuts through afflictions, ignorance, and delusions. It further means the perfection of wisdom of the understanding that brings sentient beings across the sea of suffering to the other shore. There are six versions in Chinese, individually translated into Chinese by Kumarajiva, Bodhiruci, Paramartha, Dharmagupta, Xuanzang, and Yijing.

Father and Son Sutra. Translated by Richeng of the Song dynasty.

Flower Adornment Sutra. It is one of the most important sutras of Mahayana Buddhism, and describes a cosmos of realms upon realms, mutually containing one another. The major teachings in the Huayan School are based on this sutra.

Fo Guang Dictionary. First published in 1989 in twe versions: soft cover with one index and seven volumes and hard cover with one index and three volumes. The latest edition, published in 2014, includes one index and nine volumes. All published in Taiwan by Fo Guang Cultural Enterprises Company, Ltd.

Fo Guang Textbooks. Twelve volumes, each consisting of twenty chapters, published in 1999 in Taiwan by Fo Guang Shan.

Great Compassion Dharani. This dharani has many translated versions and lengths. Regardless of the version, it is basically known as the dharani of Avalokitesvara's attainment. According to the sutras, sincerely reciting this dharani 108 times can eliminate unwholesome karma and purify the body and mind.

Great Perfection of Wisdom Treatise. The commentary on the sutra of the same name. Written by Nagarjuna and translated into Chinese by Kumarajiva in 402-405 CE. Kumarajiva was one of the four great translators for Chinese Buddhist texts. This commentary includes detailed interpretations of Buddhist doctrines, philosophies, illustrations, legends, history, geography, and rules of practice as well as the definition and function of the monastic community. Its main emphases are the philosophy and spirit of the bodhisattva path in Mahayana Buddhism and the practices of the six perfections.

Great Nirvana Sutra. There are three versions in the Chinese Buddhist canon. It offered that the Dharmakaya always abides, and that all sentient beings, including Icchantikas, possess Buddha nature and can attain Buddhahood.

Great Teacher King Sutra. Translated into Chinese by Amoghavajra.

Great Treasures Collection Sutra. The title refers to the accumulation of great Dharma treasures and innumerable methods. Its major emphasis is related to the bodhisattvas' cultivation methods and records that predicted their progress in attaining Buddhahood. The methods include the teachings and practices of emptiness, and the Pure Land and Esoteric schools.

Illuminating Light Sutra. Written by Dharmatrata and translated into Chinese by Zhu Fonian during the Yao Qin dynasty. This sutra elaborates on the concepts of impermanence, cultivation through upholding precepts, practicing concentration, and accumulating wisdom that leads to liberation, all of which are expressed through parables.

Inspiration for the Bodhicitta Pledge. The work of Master Xingan of the Qing dynasty. A list of ten causes and conditions that give rise to bodhicitta.

Lankavatara Sutra. Translated by Gunabhadra in 443 CE. It is a representation of Mahayana sutras during the latter period of Indian Buddhism. Its premise is that the existence of all phenomena is the result of the mind and its activities. It also emphasizes that the root of delusions originates from habitual tendencies and not awakening to all dharmas is the result of one's mind.

Lion's Roar of Queen Srimala Sutra. This sutra is expounded by Srimala, the daughter of King Prasenajit of Sravasti. The main points include the concept of one vehicle, the Four Noble Truths, Dharmakaya, and Buddha nature. It also describes Srimala as making ten promises and three great vows in front of the Buddha. This sutra is example of the sutras presented by a layperson. Like the *Vimalikirti Sutra*, it is also an authoritative text stating that a woman can become a Buddha.

Lotus Sutra. Following the Buddha's awakening, he first taught the *Flower Adornment Sutra*, but only the great bodhisattvas, such as Avalokitesvara and Manjusri, were able to understand. Therefore through the turning of the Dharma wheel, the Buddha expounded the Dharma, gradually moving from the essential and conventional teachings toward more advanced and transcendental teachings. He spent forty-nine years teaching the Dharma, recorded in a variety of sutras, to over three hundred assemblies, finally approaching the perfect teachings contained in the *Lotus Sutra* and the *Great Nirvana Sutra*. The Buddha only appeared in the world to teach sentient beings to awaken to the Buddha's knowledge and vision and have confidence that they, too, can become Buddhas.

Middle Way Treatise. Written by Nagarjuna, and translated into Chinese by Kumarajiva. It focuses on the wisdom and the inherent emptiness of dependent origination, and its aim is to subdue wrong views and promote right views.

Miscellaneous Treasures Sutra. Translated into Chinese by Kinkara and Tanyao. It is a collection of stories on the Buddha and his disciples, as well as important events that occurred following the Buddha's final nirvana.

Necklace of Original Conduct Sutra. Translated into Chinese by Zhu Fonian in 376-378 CE. The main contents describe the bodhisattva stages and methods of upholding and practicing the precepts to benefit sentient beings.

Numerical Discourses. Translated into Chinese by Qutan Sengqie Tipo. Compared with other *Agama Sutras*, it is the most recent, and it embraces the Mahayana philosophy.

Origins of the Vinaya Treatise. Provides descriptions of the monastic rules and governance. Includes etiquette for all monastic affairs.

Principles of the Six Perfections Sutra. Translated into Chinese by Prajna in 788 CE. This sutra describes how to protect the nation and how to practice the six perfections of the bodhisattva's cultivation.

Rice Stalk Sutra. An analogy of the twelve links of dependent origination.

Selected Chinese Buddhist Texts in Contemporary Chinese. 132 volumes, published in 1998 in Taiwan by Fo Guang Shan.

Stages of Yogacara Practice Treatise. Discoursed by Maitreya Bodhisattva, recorded by Asanga and translated into Chinese by Xuanzang. Basic text for the Yogacara School and the most important teaching in the Mind-Only School. It is also known as the *Commentary of the Seventeen Stages.*

Surangama Sutra. Translated into Chinese by Pramiti in 705 CE. A very important text for meditation practitioners. The methods of meditative concentration and the bodhisattva path are both discussed in this sutra.

Teachings Bequeathed by the Buddha Sutra. Translated into Chinese by Kumarajiva. Describes the last teachings of the Buddha before he entered final nirvana. The teachings instruct the disciples to follow the precepts, see them as their teacher, rely on them for guiding the five sense organs, and to practice diligently to attain liberation.

Twelve Divisions for the Sutras. The twelve categories of the Buddha's teachings from the collection of discourses in the Buddhist canon, classified by form and content: (1) discourses, (2) repeated verses, (3) prophesies, (4) verses, (5) unprompted teachings, (6) exposition of causes, (7) parables, (8) stories of the disciples' previous lives, (9) stories of the Buddha's previous lives, (10) profound teachings, (11) miracles, and (12) debated interpretations about the nature of all dharmas and meanings.

Vigilance for All Monastics. The original edition was authored by Zexian during the Song dynasty and later revised and recompiled in the Yuan dynasty by Yongzhong of the Linji School. A third revision was completed by Rujin. It includes over 170 key phrases of the virtuous monastics.

Vimalakirti Sutra. The main purposes of this sutra are to clarify the methods of practice for liberation that Vimalakirti achieved and to explain the practices of Mahayana bodhisattvas and the virtues that the layperson should fulfill.

Donors

2,000 copies   IBPS Hsi Lai Temple

500 copies   Jia Peir Wang & Yueh Chin Hsu Wang

100 copies   Vancouver IBPS、Min Shun S. Chang & Jia Bee Chang、Echo Tsai、Vic Wu & Chu Wu

50 copies   IBPS Austin、IBPS South Bay、Light of Buddha Temple, Inc.

25 copies   王春玲、Eva Chen

20 copies   甘萬吉

12 copies   Esther Man

10 copies   妙西法師、慧宣法師、慧軒法師、何宗霖、陳憲美、劉亞華

8 copies   李兆和、黃伯斯、Yao Wen Yeh

6 copies   Jessica Hsieh

5 copies   心古法師、依勤法師、智倫法師、王沈碧琴、張李文貞、陳李玉雙、孔祥泰、王水村、王勃鈞、王國明、呂東青、呂東堯、呂東舜、

呂銘琪、吳如意、梁蓮鳳、黃麗香、喬愛仙、曾美玉、詹瑞鄉、葉忠生、陳啓昌、陳祺媛、鄭明真、鄧柳針、孔健、李偉、俞源、Helen Chow、Angel Hsiao、Emily Liu、WaiHeong Loke、Louvenia Ortega、Bruce Zhao

3 copies　王建華、朱珠龍、林錦華、金家正、周惜賢、張美燕、張美鳳、黃少芬、黃少玲、葉彩蓮、萬小平、羅幼水、Aiden Ho、Caden Ho、Justin Yap、Tiffany Yap

2 copies　林陳雲香、朱祥華、朱祥盛、李可晴、李思彤、李浩威、李敏欣、李捷萍、林香玉、林風宏、林慧玲、林慧萍、林慧雯、郭林子、Angel Tung、Annie Wang

1 copy　心悅法師、張蘇明明、陳邱碧連、王長有、李如炎、李如珍、李如淦、李楚英、李楚洲、李楚威、張世濱、張吉祥、張坤玲、張昭蔭、張培鈴、張榮順、張福慧、黃謹雅、曾國慈、莊清池、莊麗美、郭建中、郭素薇、陳永和、陳秀娥、陳吳流、陳南宏、陳玟媛、陳姿瑾、陳星學、陳育才、陳育成、陳振聲、陳嘉成、陳豪恩、陳麗蝶、陳藝涵、鄭惠梅、李萍、陳儀、Tiffany Chang、Katherine Eng、Philip Lee、Isabell Taing、Mimi Yip、Tommy Yip

Thank you to all who donated to support the
printing and distribution of this book